"TO BE A BELIEVER IS TO BE A SPIRITUAL COLUMBUS"

Mort Crim speaks of a very old—yet very new—Christianity, a faith that calls for far more than mere church attendance. His faith demands of the church that it grow, become responsive to the needs of 20th-century men.

> **"This book by a radio and television newsman is the best work on the relation of Christianity to the problems of our time that I have read. . . . it woke me up mentally and, I believe, also spiritually. . . . LIKE IT IS! has the genius of motivating the reader to start asking questions of himself, real and searching questions."**
>
> **—Norman Vincent Peale**

LIKE IT IS!

Mort Crim

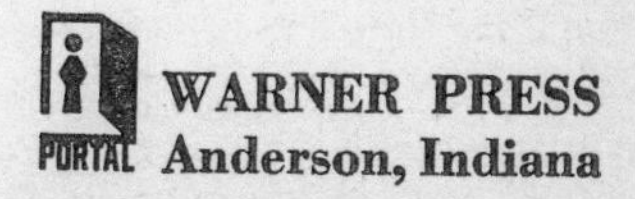

WARNER PRESS
Anderson, Indiana

To Mother and Dad
with gratitude
for
your faith in me

LIKE IT IS!

A PORTAL BOOK
Published by Pyramid Publications for Warner Press, Inc.

Portal Books edition published February, 1972

Library of Congress Catalog Card Number: 77-87325

Printed in the United States of America

PORTAL BOOKS are published by Warner Press, Inc.
1200 East 5th Street, Anderson, Indiana 46011, U.S.A.

Acknowledgments

Special thanks to my wife, Naomi, for her understanding during the long year when my every spare minute went into creation of this book. Her assistance in research, editing, and typing the final manuscript, was invaluable. And to my colleague, Steve Bell, for his frank and honest opinions, suggestions, and criticisms—all of which I solicited. Finally, to all the people whose lives throughout the years have touched mine and made it richer.

Beverly Van Poelvoorde
Myers 119 Ext 451

1. Preface (12-24)
2. pp 24-30
3. pp 31-39
4. pp 39-51
5. pp 51-61
6. pp 61-65
7. pp 66-73 10/25
8. pp 74-84 11/2
9. pp 85-95
10. pp 95-103
11. pp 104-108
12. pp 109-116
13. pp 116-126

Contents

Introduction

When Mort Crim wrote asking me to prepare a brief introduction for his new book, *Like It Is!* I was off on a long trip around the world, including a special Presidential request to visit Vietnam to speak to the troops and visit the wounded in the hospitals.

Accordingly, deadline time was at hand when I returned. I requested a ten-day extension and took the manuscript home with me, intending to read it piecemeal between times. But little did I reckon with its power-packed pages. The material gripped me so tenaciously that I read on until the early morning hours; indeed until I had finished it in its entirety! This, I assure you, is for me a rare experience! I read not a few manuscripts and books and have no trouble at all putting most aside when bedtime comes. But this one left me practically no sleeping time. In fact it woke me up mentally and I believe also spirtually.

I will go even further. Mort Crim's book literally shook me up. It challenged me personally and really made me face up to myself, to my attitudes and my participation in the great social movements of our time. *Like It Is!* has the genius of motivating the reader to start asking questions of himself, real and searching questions.

This book by a radio and television newsman is the best work on the relation of Christianity to the problems of our time that I have read. Crim carries the torch for a socially integrated Christianity, but does it so persuasively that even though he challenges the inertia and the prejudices of the reader, he does it on a rational, reasonable, and persuasive basis. But he pulls no punches about what real Christians should be thinking and doing to correct the injustices of this era. You may not entirely agree with the author's views. But how can any man's mind grow and mature on the soft mental fare of agreement?

Parting company with the ministry due to the rigid traditionalism and institutionalism which cramped him, Crim left the pastorate to enter news broadcasting in which he has had conspicuous success. But Mort Crim still sees the values in individual life changing. He did not become bitter nor turn against the church as some do. On the contrary, he merely shifted from the pulpit to the pew. He wants the church to find itself in our generation, to burst out of its old forms of thought and practice, and to become identified with the needs of people in the streets, in the ghettos, in racial distress and, indeed, to exercise a true ministry of reconciliation.

I would recommend that pastors read and study Mr. Crim's book and make copies available to their officials, leaders and members. Discussion groups built around it will stimulate creative thinking about the role of the church and of individual members.

The book will, of course, agitate the minds of some, but since when wasn't it a good thing to give one's mind an agitation treatment? I have read other books in which the author resented the church and fell upon it vindictively and even vitriolically. Such emotionalism siphons off thought value even though the author's point of view may have merit. Mr. Crim, on the contrary, has written a positive and powerful document, one that could very well be a trumpet to awaken all of us in the church and cause us to become Christ's kind of people.

It is said that an author once came to J. M. Barrie with a manuscript and asked suggestions for a title. According to the story as I heard it, Barrie asked, "Are there any bells in it?"

"No bells!" replied the author.

"Does it have any trumpets in it?" he asked, to which he received a negative reply.

"Well then," snapped Barrie, "Call it, 'No Bells, No Trumpets.' "

Mort Crim's book is packed full of ringing bells and sounding trumpets. It is written in plain, crisp newsman's language and shows amazing background and know-how. It is an inspired Christian action document for our time. Read it. It can change your life and through you, it can help change the life of this troubled, mixed-up world. In a word, this book will, as they say, "turn you on."

NORMAN VINCENT PEALE

Preface

Nearly two thousand years ago a young radical stepped into history with a message so vital it has been known ever since simply as "the gospel." This young visionary was a genius at seeing the potential in a man or woman or situation. He never overlooked what was; yet he always looked beyond to what could be.

To those who mourned man's future, he said, "Because I live, you also will live." He taught that in the ultimate economy of existence, good finally will overcome evil. Life will overcome death. He taught that men and societies can be changed. He taught that every person has intrinsic value, that every individual has ultimate worth.

To those who found life totally frustrating or unbearably boring, he announced that life could be meaningful and vibrant. To those drifting aimlessly in a sea of intellectual confusion, he proclaimed that life could be purposeful. To the sick, he offered health. To the slave, he promised freedom.

It wasn't only what he said that attracted people to his way. It was what he was. It was what he did, how he lived, how he loved. It was how he died and how he conquered death.

Jesus not only told it like it was, he showed how it ought to be. Everyone who would follow his way is compelled to do likewise. This is easier to say than to do.

Whatever profession I would pursue, I knew from the beginning I would have to perform.

Show business had an early attraction for me. Two of my aunts had been successful in vaudeville and I seemed to have a natural flair for the dramatic (including my ability to embellish even the most simple *true* story).

But, as a minister's son in a church which frowned on the theater, whatever ambition I had for the Great White Way was not encouraged. As I look back on my teen-age years, it seems to me my journey into the ministry was mostly a matter of following the path of least resistance. This is not to say I felt the ministry unimportant. I believed in it then and I do now. It is simply to say that my own involvement with the pulpit came more from circumstances than from personal convictions.

Being something of a ham, I was delighted to accept when first invited to speak in my father's church. I was fourteen at the time. It was National Youth Week, and even though the other speakers were older than I, my special status as a P.K. (preacher's kid) seemed to justify special consideration. I certainly considered that first sermon more than simply a performance. I took the speaking challenge seriously and worked hard to make my remarks meaningful.

Sadly, I have since discovered they were not. An aging wire recording of that fledgling attempt to preach confirms how lacking it was in logic if not in luster. Nonetheless, friends and family lost no time in encouraging their budding prophet.

Not that I needed encouragement. Broadway and Hollywood were emotionally as far from our church in Ohio as they were geographically. Dad's pulpit was accessible. Here, then, was my stage. It provided the dual advantage of satisfying my need to perform while at the same time pleasing parents and friends. By becoming a minister I would continue a long family tradition.

By the time I was in high school, invitations to speak at neighboring churches were numerous. Sometimes they came from neighboring states. As a teen-ager with an aptitude for public speaking, a religious background of unquestioned orthodoxy, and a last name which was reasonably well-known and respected within our church group, I soon found myself something of a contemporary circuit rider—a sort of Billy Graham with pimples.

Before I was out of high school, I was booking not only youth rallies and state youth conventions, but was frequently asked to address adult services. On numerous occasions I was invited to substitute for ministers—mostly friends of my dad—when they were absent from their pulpits.

Thus, what many young men would have been forced to learn in seminary, I began to learn before college. I was intimately familiar with the minister's life and duties, from living room to hospital room. I accompanied my father, on occasion, during calls on parishioners and I watched his actions and manner both in and out of the pulpit.

These early experiences, and my eager exploitation of them, led to early ordination. Even before I was educationally qualified, my church gave me full ministerial authority and recognition. Implicit in my ordination was an understanding that I would continue to study and would eventually fully qualify myself for the solemn responsibilities inherent in the ministerial calling.

I do not believe my relatives pulled strings or exerted pressure to accomplish this premature ordination (although I have never specifically asked them). But their standing within the church certainly did not hinder the process.

Shortly after ordination I accepted the call to pastor a church in Missouri. Through a combination of resident, extension, and correspondence courses, I continued my secular and theological studies while serving as a full-time minister. Two years later I left the pastorate to enroll as a full-time ministerial student.

During this period I began to have serious doubts about my choice of vocations. With the issue still unresolved, I accepted a call to become a pastor in northern Indiana and transferred my studies to a university nearby.

By this time I was married, and my wife (also the product of a minister's home) was fully aware of my occupational frustrations. Our two years in Indiana were both busy and decisive; for it was there that I finally resolved to leave the ministry and become a newsman.

I have mixed memories of those years—memories of counseling confused young people, troubled mothers and fathers, concerned churchmen who wanted to know how their lives could be more meaningful and how they could better serve others. The satisfactions of such work were marred by recognition of my own inadequacies—both in temperament and in training.

I remember taking the Communion cup to the ill and the elderly. I spent long nights in hospital rooms with the sick and the dying. I preached funerals, officiated at weddings, dedicated babies, and performed many other tasks which bring the clergyman into intimate contact with the most meaningful and emotional experiences of life.

Those were years when I served as chaplain to the local chapter of the Civil Air Patrol; when I played piano for our Kiwanis Club; when I helped the club wash cars to raise money for underprivileged children.

I remember with delight those situations where I was

able to help. But I remember with some dismay those situations which were beyond my capabilities. How sharply aware I became that good intentions and good background do not make a minister any more than they make a brain surgeon. I had the flair, but not the calling. I had the knack, but not the knowledge. I knew something was missing. A very important piece of the equation simply wasn't there. It was evident that what I was doing did not seem to grow out of what I was.

Toward the end of our second year in that pastorate the long-standing doubts about my vocational choice reached a climax. I want to put those doubts into proper perspective: I had not lost my faith in God, although I was quite unsure about my own concept of God. I was disturbed by some of the small and restrictive ways some churchmen seemed to view God. I was quite unhappy with the exclusive claim some Christians seemed to make on God.

I was impatient with narrow-mindedness, disgusted with dogmatism, and convinced that many of the church's practices and ideas needed a general overhaul. Still, I had not despaired of the ministry as a meaningful profession. It was a question of whether my contribution to the church and to society at large could best be made in the pulpit or out of it.

Such problems are not easily resolved by a young person who, from the cradle, has been sensitized to the "irrevocability" of the divine call. Although I could intellectually dismiss as superstition most of the stories I'd heard about dire consequences befalling men who turned from that call, emotionally I could not so easily dismiss them. Before I was old enough to read, my bedtime stories had included the saga of Jonah, who ignored God's call to preach and got swallowed by a whale. No doubt a competent psychiatrist could have untangled some of these emotional hang-ups for me.

The point is, my intellect had long since admitted that I was miscast in the role of a clergyman. My emotions had not yet accepted it and the conflict between reason and feeling kept me awake many nights.

Again and again I examined and reexamined my deepest motives. If I really wanted to leave the ministry, I had to be certain this desire for change was not merely undisciplined ego. I had to know that selfishness and greed were not at the source.

If I were challenging the validity of my call to be a minister, it had to be a valid challenge. It had to be a moral challenge. I had to know I was leaving the wrong profession for the right reasons, not leaving the right profession for the wrong ones.

I doubt that I fully understood then as well as I do now the conflict of emotions and feelings which harassed me. In retrospect I think I was beginning to see that what one does cannot substitute for what one is. I was learning that the void in a life which has not come to terms with itself can never be filled with good deeds.

Equally important to my spiritual maturity, I think I was beginning to recognize that the ministry—as Jesus practiced it and taught it—is a function of all Christians, not the private domain of a few professionals. In essence, the ministry is as simple and as universal as offering a cup of water, bandaging a wound, offering sympathy and understanding to another person. The ministry is helping others. It is being a good neighbor. It is being a friend. It is being *there* when you are needed.

It became clear to me that, by this definition, ministers were needed in all areas of life and in many vocations, wearing many titles, marching under a variety of banners.

Then one Sunday afternoon, after my wife and I had taken a group of church young people to a regional youth rally, I confronted that moment of truth which forced me to a final decision. I had grappled with—and disposed of—all the reasonable excuses for delaying an answer. What would my friends and family think? I knew that no longer mattered. What really mattered was what God would think of my decision—and what I ultimately would think of it.

There had been practical as well as moral considerations. By this time I was twenty-three and had enjoyed a selective service deferment because of my status both as a student and as minister. To resign my church and yield my ordination would mean military service almost immediately. I knew that didn't really matter, either. Perhaps a hitch in the service would give me additional time and opportunity to straighten out remaining mental and emotional tangles. (As it turned out, I am convinced my four years in the Air Force did exactly that.)

The decision to quit the ministry would mean redirecting my college and university studies. It would mean leaving the safety of a familiar environment to plunge into the competitive climate of the unknown. I had no contacts of any consequence and few friends in broadcasting.

I also had disposed of those nagging doubts about my true motives. I had faced up to those things which disturbed me about the church. I felt that some of the supposedly sacred tenets of the church were really rather useless—hardly more than crutches used to prop up a shaky faith. I seriously doubted that God was as concerned with the name which identified our sanctuary as we seemed to be. Had I remained a minister, I doubtlessly would have been branded a theological liberal. That would have been all right, for the church—like society—needs both the challenger and the protector, the innovator and the defender. Healthy tensions of this sort can make the church vital and responsive.

The important thing was I knew I was not leaving the ministry in bitterness or in disillusionment. I recognized full well my need for intellectual freedom, a freedom I was not at all sure the pastorate could provide. That may have been premature and erroneous judgment, for I know ordained ministers who seem unrestrained in exercising freedom of thought. Nonetheless, I did not exit the ministry in disgust or in despair. I could say with Ernest Harrison in Pierre Berton's book that "the Church matters. It matters enough to join, and it matters enough to leave. It is worth criticizing and it is worth supporting. It is neither an escape nor an outdated joke."

When the moment of separation came, I left in the calm and quiet assurance that my contribution, whatever it would be, could best be made in a secular context.

My final Sunday as a pastor was a sad day, yet it was a day of liberation. Like a school commencement, it marked a new beginning but it was necessarily interwoven with nostalgia. In that last sermon I would ever preach as an ordained minister, I declared my independence to be a whole person, a free man, a seeker after life without regard to how such a quest might affect my status in the church. It was a commitment to truth no matter what the consequences.

I did not feel I was leaving the church—only its confines. In a sense, I did not feel I was renouncing the ministry—only the ministerial profession. I was not forsaking the sanctuary, merely transferring from pulpit to pew. I expected that the studio would, perhaps, be an extension of the study.

Occasionally these days I return to the pulpit—not as a minister, but as a layman. I speak as a newsman, discussing this difficult and dangerous world of ours from the Christian perspective. It is a comfortable role now. I feel much more at home as a guest in the pulpit than I ever did as a resident.

There is no lack of opportunity for anyone today who is willing to serve his fellowman. In my vocation, and in countless other secular pursuits, the needs are painfully visible. Sometimes we laymen can step through doors of opportunity rarely—if ever—opened to the professional clergyman. While I no longer officiate at weddings, bury the dead, or break communion bread, I am perhaps more qualified now to perform acts no less holy: such as introducing meaning into a life that has none; introducing God to a person who—because of prejudice, pride or guilt—would never discuss such matters with a minister.

Remember, by vocation Jesus was a carpenter. Most of his life was spent in a woodworking shop.

Paul was a professional tentmaker. According to the New Testament, he never gave up that secular vocation. What Paul did for a living never interfered with what he was in life.

It is great when *doing* and *being* converge for a person as they now do for me. I find being a Christian and doing my job as a journalist not only compatible but increasingly related. I am learning, every day, what the late Dag Hammarskjold must have meant when he said, "In our era, the road to holiness necessarily passes through the world of action." By the time I completed graduate journalism studies, I had a firm fix on my vocational goals. The old doubts were gone, replaced by a new confidence in the future and a fresh sense of direction.

My work as both television and radio broadcaster in the post-pastoral era has been rewarding. It has included exciting stints as a local news reporter in Chicago and New York, and for the past four years now, a network correspondent's assignment with the American

Broadcasting Company. During this period our home has been blessed with a bright and healthy son for whom I pray life will get off to a less complicated start. But if it does not, then I hope he will come to the same understanding of life's meaning and beauty which finally has come to pass for his parents.

I hope he will find work which satisfies him as much as mine satisfies me. A meaningful profession, full of challenge and promise. A profession where he can serve others. Who knows? Maybe my son will become a minister. If he should take up that torch, for the right reasons and on his own terms, his mother and I would be quite pleased. Whatever his final decision, I hope I show as much love and understanding and acceptance as my parents gave to me.

As a newsman I live and work where the action is. Within an eight-month period I reported from three presidential summit conferences and traveled around the world with President Lyndon Johnson.

I've interviewed some of the most interesting, famous, and powerful people in the world. I have a front-row seat to the greatest show on earth. Early in the Gemini space flight program, I began covering manned launches from Cape Kennedy. I've been there for all the Apollo flights.

I have high hopes, big aspirations, and few regrets. I believe I have learned from the past how to make better use of the future.

Don't get the idea that being a Christian and an ex-minister make me immune to the frustrations of life. Like every other person caught up in the sound and the fury of the twentieth century, I experience moments of disappointment, anger, envy, and—sometimes—too much ambition. Like everyone else, I catch myself worrying too much. But I'm learning, day by day, how to face life with confidence and certainty. I believe my perspective is improving.

I am discovering in the laboratory of life how faith can cure frustrations; how Christian hope can alleviate disappointment; how Christian love can neutralize anger; how concern for others can temper envy and ambition.

In a world like ours, filled with so much loneliness, bitterness, unhappiness, fear, and despair, there's a big market today for people who not only tell it like it is, but who try to show how it ought to be. The market will not be adequately served from the study alone.

Chapter 1

A Happening

Since the beginning of time man has been trying to balance the books. Each generation attempts to find as many answers as there are questions and each generations fails. The compounding of problems always exceeds the income of solutions; so, each generation ends in the red, passing to the next liabilities as well as assets.

Now, for the first time in history, the liabilities threaten to wipe out the assets. This generation has been handed a promissory note which soon may have to be paid in full. It is a mortgage on life itself and there may not be time to pass it on. For this generation faces the supreme question: Can man survive? It is nothing less than whether or not man has a future. Time seems to be running out and if this account is not settled, the books may be forever closed.

The question was conceived in the splitting of an atom, born of a mushroom cloud, nurtured by a cold war, and brought to early maturity through the rapid development of military technology.

Can man survive? The question is emotional dynamite, exploding on campuses where students are convinced they cannot wait for an answer. If this issue is not resolved, nothing else matters.

Can man survive? The question shadows our hopes, haunts out dreams, and infects our relationships. It reminds us that instant annihilation is a mere push button away. But it also addresses itself to famine, overpopulation, and pollution of the environment—for death need not be instant to be certain.

Can man survive? The question is not always articulated, but it is always present—filling the atmosphere with tension, depression, and despair. We cannot avoid inhaling its poisonous implications and it stunts our growth as individuals and as a nation. The question has produced a national melancholy. One British journalist observes that the United States "sometimes seems to be on the edge of a national nervous breakdown."

There is more to man's dilemma, however, than the question of physical survival. In a world warped by hatred, where men still are despised or destroyed because of their color or their point of view; in a world torn by conflict and plagued by injustice, some may question man's right to survival.

And if man should survive, will his continuation have any ultimate meaning?

Such are the questions which disturb us. We should hardly wonder at the sadness in the land.

As a newsman whose daily job it is to chronicle man's predicament, I understand the gloom. I do not share it, for I believe something can be done and must be done by this generation.

There is an infinite power for change which man barely has tapped. For all his scienfific and technological progress, man has hardly moved beyond the first frontier of spiritual development.

I believe this generation shows signs of sensitivity to that truth. Very often these days I hear these questions: What do you know for sure? and, What does it all mean? The questions may be asked glibly, but they clearly reveal modern man's longing for meaning and certainty.

Earlier generations seemed quite capable of finding both. Why, then, has it all come unstuck for this generation? Why won't the pieces fit? Never has man known so much. Why does he seem sure of so little?

The questions of meaning and certainty are not only basic, they are universal. Every person must answer. And every person must build his life upon the answers.

According to a folk singer I heard recently on my car radio, "life is what we do while we're waiting to die."

For the writer of those lyrics, life apparently equals zero. A similar despair is reflected in many contemporary books, plays, and movies. They tell us that the pains and pleasures of life, the victories and defeats, all add up to futility.

Suicide statistics and the figures on mental breakdown seem to confirm that, for many people, life is a vapor—without meaning or value.

Modern man has discovered lots of answers, but not *the* answer. He knows much about how-to but very little about what-for. He seems more capable of extending life than of enriching it. He is long on pleasure but short on purpose.

Perhaps the fruit of knowledge has forced us out of paradise, for modern man sees his own minuteness much more clearly than his ancestors saw theirs.

Astronomy provides cosmic testimony to man's unspeakable insignificance. A look into a clear, night sky tells man how tiny he is. History shows man that his entire existence is no more than a speck on the calendar of time.

Science warns man that his planet is programmed for ultimate destruction. A comet or a fragment of the sun could end everything in a flash. Or, earth's gradual departure from the sun may someday turn the world into a celestial ice cube.

Now the "bomb" has given man the means for beating mother nature to the final punch. And, it became public knowledge only recently that the United States has developed a series of biological weapons potentially as deadly as nuclear fallout and much more difficult to detect. One virus bomb no bigger than a fruit jar reportedly could wipe out all life within a cubic mile, without warning and without remedy.

Newspaper headlines describe how a tornado ruins in a minute the town it took a century to build. Radio and television newscasts remind us of our mortality with casualty figures from floods, plane crashes, highway accidents, and Vietnam.

Heart attacks, cancer, and countless other maladies continue their grim reaping. Even in our unsure age, death is one certainty no one questions.

The fact of death is more visible and more constant today than ever before. Instant death for mankind is more probable today than ever before. Should we, therefore, be surprised by man's mood of despondency?

The problem is that most men have not resolved the ultimate question posed by death. They only know they must die. A psychiatrist-friend of mine tells me that no one enjoys complete mental health who has not come to terms with death.

It was the late Dag Hammarskjold who observed that

in the last analysis, it is our conception of death which decides our answers to all the major questions of life.

What you or I believe about the grave greatly influences what we are. Our view of the hereafter profoundly influences our actions in the here-and-now.

It is difficult to walk purposefully and confidently through life if one shares, for instance, Bertrand Russell's depressing view of man: "Man is . . . but the product of accidental colocations of atoms . . . All the noonday brightness of human genius [is] destined to ultimate extinction."[1]

Jean-Paul Sartre holds a similarly unhappy concept of what man is and where he's going when he writes about man being nothing else than his plan . . . nothing else than the ensemble of his acts . . . Man is a useless passion.[2]

Undoubtedly, Russell and Sartre tell it like it is for millions of people today.

But hear another voice—a voice telling how it can be. The late Martin Luther King, Jr., said of death: "We need not fear it. The God who brought our whirling planet from primal vapor and has led the human pilgrimage for lo these many centuries can most assuredly lead us through death's dark night into the bright daybreak of eternal life."[3]

Dr. King was a master with words, but these clearly are more than the poetic utterances of a great orator. They are the unflinching testimony of a man who found meaning in the minutes and the hours and the days of life. They reflect the personal philosophy of a man who told it like it was, but who saw beyond the reality to the possibility.

We need not be reminded that for Martin Luther King, Jr., life was much more than a fragile bridge between birth and death; much more than a shadow without substance; much more than simply something to do while waiting to die. By his own testimony, King had resolved the basic issue of death. He had come to terms with man's final encounter—and won. For him, life was a happening.

Few would accuse this modern martyr of being an impractical dreamer—a wild-eyed idealist. He had a dream and he had ideals, but he stood firmly on the solid ground of reality. He put his visions to work. His life had the sparkle of ultimate significance because, in the words of his funeral eulogy, "he knew where he came from and he knew where he was going."

History will record the greatness of Martin Luther King's works. Hopefully, history will also remember his great spirit; for he was one of those rare mortals who, in this supersophisticated era of miniature circuits and mighty moon rockets, dared to declare, "I believe."

Surely no one knows *how* to live until he first knows *why*.

Albert Einstein was only four or five years old when he watched the motion of a compass needle, and said, "Something deeply hidden has to be behind things." Einstein never lost his faith in creative purpose. In fact, as he grew to manhood and began exploring the mysteries of the universe, that faith grew. In later life, Einstein said: "My religion consists of a humble admiration for the Superior Spirit who reveals Himself in the slight details we are able to perceive with our frail and feeble minds."[4] For Einstein, life was a symmetry of significance. A happening!

Most of history's heroes have been men with deep convictions about the ultimate meaning of existence. One need not, however, be a moral giant to discover meaning. One need only confront life with intellectual honesty, humility, and sensitivity.

Why is sensitivity important? Because there are so many subtle expressions of meaning woven into the fabric of life. These intimations of ultimate purpose do not beat upon our intellects with the force of a hurricane. Rather, they stir softly, like a refreshing breeze, across the acrid pessimism of our day.

Sensitivity is important because no one can prove the existence of a great mind behind all matter—not even an Einstein. But then, many of life's most meaningful experiences are beyond the scope of scientific evidence. Would we demand proof that flowers are beautiful? That sunsets inspire? We expect no lawyer's case to be made of our love for another person, nor to prove that person loves us. The heart does, indeed, have its own reasons.

To the sensitive soul, man's exploration of the heavens is providing new intimations of creative power and purpose. Through the electronic eye of television, you and I rode with the "Snoopy" moonship down to the lunar mountaintops during the trailblazing flight of Apollo Ten. The cratered landscapes we saw spoke of frightful forces at work over billions of years. We wondered what volcanic eruptions, what bombardment by meteors, what explosions carved out such grandeur. Is it really so incredible to say, "In the beginning, God . . ."?

The most intellectually honest person must make some basic assumptions about life. Is it less honest to presume that life has ultimate meaning than to presume it does not? Is it less honest to presume that death is only a phase than to presume it is a finality? Many writers have pondered this question.

In his poem, "Johnson Over Jordan," J. B. Priestley writes, "there is in me something that will not rest until it sees Paradise . . ." and Malinowski has perhaps spoken for all mankind when he says: "Nothing really matters except the answer to the burning question, 'Am I going to live or shall I vanish like a bubble?' What is the aim and issue of all this strife and suffering?"

If life is no more than a cosmic accident, a mindless joke, a swirl of confusion and color splashed across the black backdrop of meaningless time, then perhaps the discotheque is man's truest expression of reality. There, bathed in the flashing brilliance of psychedelia, rocked by the pulsating rhythms of the electronic beat, stimulated by the sensuous gyrations of go-go dancers—there, in miniature, is the story and the glory of life.

If, however, life is the considered output of love and intellect; if human existence is the product of purpose; if life is more than something to do while waiting to die; then the truest expression of reality is man living purposefully.

The difference in viewpoint is fundamental. Either life is an illusion, a hopped-up trip, a journey without signposts down a dead-end street, or life is real, a migration toward an even greater reality, a procession of purpose.

Just as love between two people can seldom be dictated or destroyed by pure logic, so—it seems to me—one's belief in the meaning of life is seldom the product of reason only. There is a language of the soul—intuition, perhaps. It takes over at the point where logic ends. It bridges the gap between what is knowable and what is believable. When intellect has revealed to us what *is*, faith reveals to use what *can be*.

It has always been so. It was so when Moses defied the odds and led his people out of Egyptian slavery. It was so when Joan of Arc followed her "voices." It was so when Martin Luther King, Jr., marched his people down the highways toward hope. Faith continues, even now, to span the chasm between the actual and the possible.

Some cannot bring themselves to call life's ultimate source, God. The fact is that people in different lands, different cultures, and at different times in history, have used a variety of terms to describe the Deity. Perhaps we who believe are partly to blame for the present rejection of the word, God. I am convinced that what many young people today reject is not God, but caricatures of God which we unwittingly have created.

Too often we portray God as a spiritual Santa Claus who gives gifts to his *good* children; or as some sort of heavenly genie who jumps to our bidding whenever we rub the magic lamp of prayer.

Too often we have overemphasized God's role in the world while overlooking our own. We have talked much of God's will; now, perhaps it is time we talked of man's will, for God has put us in charge here. Hatred, war, selfishness, injustice, hunger—these are not God's will. They are the consequences of man's willfulness.

Too often we invite the challenge, "Well, if there is a God, and if he's supposed to be kind and loving, how can he permit suffering? How can a good God let little children starve in Biafra or be killed and orphaned in Vietnam?"

The question ignores man's obvious role in the continuing creative process. Even the earliest Scriptures clearly teach that man has been given dominion over the earth—has been charged not only with replenishing, but with tending it. God cannot deny man the right to do wrong. Such inhibitions would reduce man to the level of animals or insects. The same freedom of choice which permits a man to be noble and compassionate also allows him to be greedy and hateful.

The question also ignores an obvious law of life, one which the Christian missionary, Paul, stated this way: "Do not deceive yourselves . . . a man will reap exactly what he plants" (Gal. 6:7 TEV).[5]

Kirby Page asked why should man expect to reap brotherhood when he plants hatred? Why should he expect to reap peace when he plants injustice? Even the most illiterate sharecropper knows that when tomatoes are planted, tomatoes are harvested. Not onions. Not radishes. Tomatoes. And not half the time. Not 90 percent of the time. All the time. When an acorn falls, an oak tree grows. Not an elm, not a cedar, not a pine—but an oak.

Man fights, and man kills, and man suffers, because man continues to plant the seeds of war and misery.

If we could not discern such consistency in the affairs of nature, then we might legitimately question the existence of a purposeful creator. So what we see in man's tragic relationship to man is not a paradox at all; rather, it is confirmation that life does follow a pattern. It may sometimes be terrible or brutal, but it is seldom unpredictable, never whimsical.

There is an excitement about the words, "I believe." There is a magic quality about those words when they are spoken with conviction, for they affirm an absolute faith in the future, a faith invulnerable to the fears of the moment. They are confidence, flung into the face of terror and tragedy. They are compassion and care, tenderly poured over a world of war, starvation, and frustration.

In an era when people suffocate under the smog of hopelessness and despair, the man who has found faith breathes the clean, exhilarating air of assurance. He knows the future is not in the spastic hands of some fickle fate, some blind and mindless whim. He knows that all things, ultimately and finally are working together toward good.

The apostle Paul once said that the committed person who has hope only in this life is a most miserable person. His noblest dreams will evaporate and his finest works will turn to dust.

An alternative to such despair was handed to man hundreds of years ago on a small hillside just outside the ancient city of Jerusalem. There a symbol of one man's death became the symbol of all men's hopes. There a cross was erected. A young man was hanged on it, and the world was never again the same.

There was nothing special about that cross. Hundreds, probably thousands, of common criminals and traitors had suffered similar, humiliating deaths on similar crosses.

But the Jewish prophet they nailed up that day was somebody special. His life had been special. His death was special. His special brand of love was to become the ultimate mind-expanding power.

That cross marked the spot where history was divided into B.C. and A.D. It continues to mark the intersection at which individual lives move toward meaning or into oblivion. To fully recognize that cross is to come to terms with death—not just physical death, but death to selfishness, to fear, and to despair.

That symbol of death is equally the symbol of life; for on that cross, death was conquered by love. It is a cross with two beams: one horizontal, as though embracing all mankind in shared suffering, the other vertical, as though pointing toward ultimate meaning. The vertical beam is anchored solidly in the physical world—the here-and-now, but it directs our attention to the hereafter. Jesus' life and death give meaning to ours, in the context of eternity.

This is supposed to be the age of the happening. Yippies and hippies stage sign-in, love-ins, nude-ins, freak-outs, and pot-parties—all in the name of awareness. But, like the elusive pot of gold at the end of the rainbow, fulfillment always seems just out of reach.

Anyone who's been that way will tell you that the drug-and-sex route to reality is a blind alley. The "trips" turn out to be roller coaster rides—fast, maybe thrilling, but leading nowhere.

In the name of awareness, awareness is crushed. The senses are dulled. The mind is not expanded, rather the intellect is stunted.

Anyone who's been Christ's way will tell you that the real road to reality begins in the doorway of an empty tomb, not on the end of a needle or in a cube of LSD. The personal knowledge that Jesus has met death head-on for all of us—and won. This is what invigorates and electrifies life! This is what turns life into a happening!

The challenge of the cross demands total awareness. It insists on touching life, tasting it, grappling with it. It compels us to experience. It means being turned on. But Jesus' followers won't settle for illusion or make-believe. They must see life like it is.

To deal with life like it is demands spiritual resilience. Flexibility. For life is not static, but dynamic. Life, as Jesus lived it, was much more than going by the book. He introduced a dimension—a quality of life—which was too big to fit in a rule book. Mercy was more important to him than law; justice, more important than order.

Jesus refused to be enslaved by rigid regulations. This infuriated the religious leaders of his day. Some churchmen today are similarly outraged by a situational approach to morality. It is always easier to apply a rule than to search one's mind and heart for an answer. Recitation requires far less effort than reason. This explains, at least partly, the popular appeal of orthodoxies (religious or political) which provide packaged answers to life. Unfortunately, life provides few packaged questions.

I find it distressing that Christianity is still equated with the acceptance of certain dogmas. Throughout history Christ's followers have been recognized not so much by what they have said as by what they have done. Not promise but performance. Not adjectives but attitudes. Actions. Relationships. Life style.

Kahlil Gibran, the Lebanese mystic, wrote: "Your daily life is your temple and your religion."[6] Jesus certainly taught that rituals and observances are not substitutes for deeds. His way always leads to where the action is. It provides no emotional cocoon, no intellectual sanctuary.

Jesus had a knack for hanging around with the wrong people: the social outcasts, the mentally disturbed, the profane, the swindlers, the prostitutes. He plunged into life with vigor. Like a good physician, he went where sick people were. No isolated wards for this great healer. He never ducked danger, and his steadfast, dogged response to the challenges of human need led him to an early death.

I believe young people are indifferent to the church today—not because the church has required too much of them, but because it has demanded so little. In my travels around the country, I find American youth bored and angry. Bored with a society that's tried to take all the danger out of their lives. Angry with an establishment which has traded adventure for affluence.

Youngsters don't want their lives all plotted out in advance. Many of them, especially the brighter ones, simply are unwilling to renounce all risks in return for security. We should be grateful for a generation of youth which refuses to take the don't-rock-the-boat pledge!

Idealistic behavior by children can be very upsetting to their more pragmatic parents. Some mothers and fathers find it inconceivable that their offspring should renounce the orderly and safe lives meticulously planned for them. Why should they reject a system which trades comfort for conformity? All that's required of youth is that they hazard no bets—take no chances.

Donald Atwell Zoll believes the open rebellion by young people is partly a reaction to society's attempts to tranquilize them: "From gang rumbles to LSD trips, university riots to sex orgies, dirty words to pacifism, youth has attempted to reinstate the perennial need for danger, to strangely reassert the necessity of combat, even of outright violence, even if one does so by being violently nonviolent."

Zoll said further in this UPI interview that the only way young people can be won back is for society to reopen the opportunities for individual risk and excitement.

The kids are primed for action. They are ripe for a challenge. They will never buy a religion whose chief function is defending a document of thou-shalts and thou-shalt-nots. I believe they will be attracted to a compassionate view of life which sees the risks, the possibilities, the golden but perilous promises in the world. For this, in the words of Thomas Howard, is a "wild and elastic and moving world."[7] It's the kind of world where static moral codes just won't do. Try as we will to deny it, times have changed; the stale, often crusty, proscriptions of a simpler era have little appeal and little usefulness.

Sensitive persons today recognize that apathy is the supreme sin. The failure to care is the gravest injustice we can inflict on a fellow human—the failure to love, to act in his behalf.

Real Christianity means leaving the comfort and tranquility of the temple and moving into the world of sweat, blood, and tears.

The New Testament includes a story about Jesus and his disciples and a marvelous experience they shared on a hill called the Mount of Transfiguration. The disciples wanted to stay there, build tabernacles, and let the good times roll. Jesus wouldn't permit that. He insisted that religious insights be connected with daily lives.

The missionary, Paul, wrote what may be the closest we can come to finding a formula for Christian living:

> Love one another warmly . . . and be eager to show respect for one another. Work hard, and do not be lazy. Serve . . . with a heart full of devotion. . . . Share your belongings with your needy brothers, and open your homes to strangers. . . .
> Do not be proud but accept humble duties.
> Do not think of yourselves as wise.
> If someone does evil to you, do not pay him back with evil.
> Try to do what all men consider to be good.
> Do everything possible, on your part, to live at peace with all men—(Rom. 12:10-18 TEV).

This is a clear call to action. Verbal piety simply wasn't Paul's bag. His commitment found expression, not in the sanctuary, but in the streets. Conformity wasn't his bit, either. For Paul, Christianity meant creative response to the needs of others.

Paul knew, as we must learn, that sometimes the greatest insights come, not in burning bushes or atop mystical mountains, but in the commonplace clamor. He knew that if God is *anywhere*, he is *everywhere*.

God may be found in a church building, but he also may be felt in the art gallery, the museum, or along the assembly line.

God may be heard in the singing or a hymn, but he also may be sensed in the performance of a musical masterpiece or the singing of a folk sing.

God may speak through the Bible or a book of theology, but he also may say something to us through the newspaper, radio and television, the voice of a friend, the anguished sob of a young widow, or the tormented cry of a dope addict.

God may reveal himself through the life of a believer, but he also may communicate through the desperate dialogue of a play or a book. Even that dramatic or literary work which mocks God may speak volumes about the loneliness and despair of troubled men—men he created; men he loves.

I have found deep, religious experiences in secular books such as *To Kill a Mockingbird,* or movies like "Guess Who's Coming to Dinner." How wrong it is to segregate life—to compartmentalize life into categories, saying of one activity, "This is religious," and of another, "This is secular." How wholly artificial.

I welcome—indeed, I demand—every experience which makes my fellow human more knowable and which makes me more aware. I must see life like it is—the good. The bad. And the ugly.

Chapter 2

Let's Have a Love-in

A sign in a Greenwich Village shop reads: "I love humanity, it's people I can't stand."

That simple slogan speaks volumes about the love problem today. It is easy to love in general. To love specifically is something else.

We may, for instance, love the Negro race, but find it difficult to love the black man who moves his family in next door.

The true test of love is how a person reacts in specific

situations. Theoretical love is irrelevant. To be valid, love must come into focus in particular situations.

Love is a very big word today. It is a much misunderstood word. It is a much misused word. The flower children have declared it, but many of them have failed to comprehend it. Many have learned that love, misunderstood, can produce devastating disillusionment.

In the words of Christopher Rhodes, a hippie in Boston, "This love bit is losing some of its innocence. When you're hungry and you've got bugs on you and no place to take a bath, you don't feel much like loving people anymore."

No matter how much this word love has been abused, it remains at the heart of the Christian faith. Christians are called to be lovers.

Remember that song "The Old Time Religion"? Remember the part that asserts "It makes me love everybody"? That was a worthy sentiment. It had the ring of companionship and togetherness, but it wasn't always true. Sometimes the churchgoers who sang that part the loudest loved the least. Often they didn't even realize their lack of compassion.

Of course they loved their neighbors. It was simply that when they got down to specifics, some of them were rather finicky about whom they were willing to call neighbors.

Charles V. Glock recently said that studies show Christian laymen—as a group—to be a rather prejudiced lot. Glock claims the majority of laymen want their churches to attend to private religious needs of members, and stay out of such questions as peace, social justice, and human rights.

For example, Glock says that in 1967, a national opinion research center poll showed 89 percent of the Christian laity interviewed felt negroes should take advantage of the opportunities society already offers and stop protesting. He says 70 percent of the laymen interviewed renounced clerical involvement in social issues such as civil rights.[1]

This is sad, because it is in the arena of personal relations and human contact that the love ethic of Jesus is put to the test.

When the chief priests and scribes asked Jesus which of the 613 commandments he considered the most important, he said, "This is the most important one . . . 'you must love the Lord your God with all your heart, and with all your soul, and with all your mind, and with all your strength.' The second most important commandment is this: 'You must love your neighbor as yourself.' There is no other commandment more important than these two" (Mark 12:29-31 TEV).

In other words, Jesus was saying that it's just as important to love our fellowmen as it is to love God. The pharisees considered this nothing short of blasphemy. Too many church leaders today are similarly upset by this demanding gospel of love.

It's a dangerous gospel, too, when we begin to apply it to specific areas of conflict and unrest in social life.

I once heard an ex-governor describe his successor as a "man with a blue pencil where his heart ought to be." He was simply saying that this man seemed more interested in balancing budgets than in helping people.

The continuing argument over whether the church should be concerned with saving souls or saving bodies has always seemed to me a senseless debate. It is much like the national controversy over guns versus butter. It is just as stupid to suppose that a nation can afford to drop all its defenses as it is to believe that a nation can ignore its internal problems. The fact is a nation must meet both its external as well as its internal responsibilities. It is not an either/or situation.

Whatever debate goes on should concern the degree

or the emphasis to be given each—not whether one should be of exclusive concern. The church ministers to the hunger of both mind and stomach. An Associated Press dispatch quoted F. Donald Coggan, archbishop of York, addressing a meeting in Uppsala, as saying, "I am oppressed by the appalling realities of the population explosion. The solemn threat [is] that by the year 2,000, the world population is likely to be practically doubled." He went on to say, "I think in terms not only of body-hunger, but of mind- and soul-hunger when I ponder these figures." He concluded, "The church must always go on her mission in the world with the Bible in her hand."

Perhaps another way of saying this is to reiterate a fundamental truth about the Christian gospel: It is the gospel of the whole man. It speaks to man's spiritual and emotional as well as to his physical needs. The church today, if it is to be relevant in our kind of world, must stop looking at man in an either/or fashion. It must stop seeing man as either physical or spiritual. The church must reclaim Jesus' own concept that man is both.

The Apollo Eleven moon landing has proven conclusively that this nation can achieve almost any goal to which it assigns a sufficiently high priority. It cost the United States more than $24 billion to pave that celestial highway linking the Atlantic Ocean with the Sea of Tranquility. Our experts tell us that hunger could be eliminated as a major problem in America for about $2.5 billion. Even that sounds like a lot of money until we realize that Americans are spending $2 billion a year to house, care for, and feed their pets, and that figure is growing fast.

It is estimated there are at least three times the number of domesticated animals in the United States as there are people. Do we as a nation really care more about our dogs, cats, birds, fish, turtles, and monkeys, than we do about people?

Americans show signs of weariness with the frequent and seemingly repetitious calls for benevolence. This is not a new phenomenon, for the needs are always with us. The early church faced the same temptation and Paul addressed himself to this problem when he wrote to the Christians in Galatia nineteen centuries ago, "Let us not become tired of doing good."

A perceptive observer said recently he thinks many Americans who are essentially kind and decent people are simply suffering from "compassion fatigue."

That catchy phrase implies a condition in which our capacity for sympathy is exhausted by overuse. And yet, love and concern are so crucial to the Christian reality and so vital to salvaging wasted humanity that we must not tire of doing good. Jesus was in the business of reclaiming people—saving lost lives. Of course he reclaimed individuals. He rescued at the personal level.

But in our complex and populous society, there is a broader responsibility. We must remember that Jesus not only saved from the spiritual slavery of selfishness and meaninglessness, but he fed the hungry and healed the sick. The Christian's task, therefore, is not only to introduce purpose and meaning and the power to overcome in life. The job includes feeding the hungry, sheltering the homeless, caring for the ill. This is not a question of political philosophy. It is not a question of competing systems of government. For the Christian, it is a question of people-orientation. What do we care about most? Programs? Property? Or people?

Too often the church has, by neglect and indifference, given the wrong answer. Remember that the rich young ruler was all excited about Jesus until Jesus told him to sell everything he had and give the income to the poor. Then, like many of us, he turned and went away sorrowful.

Donald Reed writes:

> How roundly Jesus condemns the deep blasphemy of our slick preoccupation with 'problems'; when all the time there are no such things as 'problems'; there are only people, people in need. A preoccupation with problems is one of the occupational diseases of being a Christian in the modern world. A propensity for shutting ourselves off from reality behind a smoke-screen of words is the most insidious of the many sins that so easily beset us.[2]

In an article entitled, "God's Little People," Ernest T. Campbell says, "The hungry, the thirsty, the home-less, the sick, the naked, the imprisoned—this is our docket. They are our mission."[3]

Then Campbell goes on to outline how we Christians can go about the work of caring for God's little people —the casualties of life. People who are not big in power, big in attractiveness, big in reputation, but who are big with God. He suggests three ways:

First, the way of personal helpfulness. That is, on a man-to-man basis. As Wordsworth put it, those "little, nameless, unremembered acts of kindness and love." Remember that outsiders used to say of the early Chris-tians, "Behold, how they love one another."

The second way Christians minister to God's little people can be termed the way of organized benevo-lence. Campbell says because many of man's needs are repetitive, we have established a network of welfare agencies and service organizations. For instance, if one girl comes to the city from the farm each month, we ar-range for a family in the city to take her in. But when 500 girls come to the city from the farm each month, the answer is to organize a YWCA.

Then Campbell comes to the third way by which Christians help God's little people. That is by lifting hand and voice to "change the structures in our common life that produce the hungry, the thirsty, the naked, the homeless, and the imprisoned." This means that love works through the Christian, not only at the personal level, not only at the intimate group level, but at the social and political levels as well. It means Christian love is expressed not only in small acts of personal kindness, but in the ballot box when a vote is registered for open housing, for better schools, for more meaningful and efficient welfare programs. Gandhi probably was the first man in history to fully understand how Jesus' love ethic could be applied at the social as well as at the individual level. Martin Luther King, Jr., understood, too.

America needs a love-in—a massive and relentless demonstration by the church that it does indeed care. Not words. Not platitudes. But action. Love that lifts. This is the need.

Like the twenty students at Creighton University in Omaha who have been writing to and visiting inmates at the Nebraska state reformatory and penitentiary. These kids have launched a program they hope will reduce the chances of inmates going back to prison. Student leaders call their project the University of the Streets.

This kind of program has a biblical basis. Too often we forget Jesus' parable about the man who stood before the bar of eternal justice pleading his case as a good and faithful servant, only to be challenged by the Almighty for having failed—among other things—to care for those in prison.

According to a leader of the Creighton project, the student's concern will not end when an inmate is released. A student will be available to him as a person. Not as a counselor, but as a friend. They may attend a group meeting, or go bowling. It's a contact to meet people, to fill an evening. These students at Creighton demonstrate that free and unselfish spirit which seems to be built-in to many college people today. They seem to be showing an attitude of accepting others for what they are. A lot of them, willingly dedicating themselves to a human cause.

Christian concern, of course, must not stop there. What about prison reform? What about the inhuman treatment countless prisoners in many institutions receive because of insufficient budgets, ill-trained personnel, or apathy on the part of the general populace? What about the social conditions which breed crime, and antiquated court systems which deal inadequately and often unfairly with the criminal and the accused criminal? Christian duty demands concern for the individual prisoner. But Christian duty also demands action to overhaul or even replace within society those structures which contribute to the problem of crime.

The organized church is not always the first to offer a rescuing hand. Consider what some hippies have done in San Francisco. They've launched a project called Switchboard. It's a telephone information service which people can call day or night to find answers to their problems. Any problems. If the volunteer workers at Switchboard don't have the solution, they chat about it for awhile. Then they seek answers from anyone who might know. That could be a minister, a doctor, a psychiatrist, a sociologist, or even another person with a similar problem. Switchboards are now being organized in other cities, including Washington, D.C.; Seattle; Columbus, Ohio; Montreal; Berkeley, and Oakland, California.

The first Switchboard was set up in the Haight-Ashbury district of San Francisco by the flower children themselves, to provide some help for tens of thousands of alienated youths who flooded that district in the summer of 1967. While much of organized religion criticized the hippie movement, some hippies launched do-it-yourself operations to transmit messages, calm people on bad LSD trips, keep track of cheap places to eat, advise runaway children, list jobs, and catalog housing. In a real sense, they filled a vacuum which should have challenged the church to an immediate response. Here was an authentic mission field. Many churchmen—though there were some notable exceptions—failed to recognize it.

Some of the Switchboard callers are lonely. Some are in genuine personal trouble. Some are people perplexed by the problems of a complex, computerized, impersonal society. Wouldn't it be great if the church had this kind of hot line to human need?

Love is a tough word. It's not some nebulous, passive, sentimentality. It's not a Boy Scout oath or a pledge of allegiance. Christian love is all-compelling, all-consuming. It can cleanse us of selfishness, purge us of prejudice, and transform our indifference into a passionate concern. Christian love goes to work.

A man signed his name with an X when he applied for a job—Chrysler Corporation hired him and found he was an outstanding worker. Then there was the man who was hung-up over his prison record; his inability to pass an employment test; and the fact that he was black. He applied for a job at Ford Motor Company, was hired, and within eight months had been promoted twice.

There was "Spike," who went to work at General Motors. Spike said his only income until that time came from "craps, women, and peddling drugs."

These three men, and some ten thousand others, came to the auto giants from the hangdog army of the hard-core unemployed. The unemployables. Some had worked perhaps eleven months in their lives. Some had spent as long as twenty-six years in jail. Still others had neither prison records nor work records.

Under the old system of screening and testing, the automobile industry and most others had no place for them. But under a program pushed by the National Alliance of Businessmen, the auto companies gave no tests, ignored the prison records, and went into the ghettos to hire men instead of waiting for the men to come out of the ghettos to the plant gates.

What are the results? One year after the program was initiated, it was clear the hard rocks from the hard corps were staying on the job as long as—or longer than—men hired through normal channels. In the words of one automotive executive, "Once they've been on the job for awhile and get used to working, we've got no more problems with them than with the other men. And they definitely begin to show a self-pride they hadn't shown before."

That is love on the assembly line. That is love at work, not the mere mouthing of sentiment. Such love, of course, implies risk. For to love is always to take a chance. To commit yourself to someone else and to permit that person to become an integral part of yourself is to make yourself extremely vulnerable to the cold hand of fate. There are those who cannot love or will not take the chance. They may fear rejection, or failure, or betrayal.

I thought of the terrible risk of loving as I waited at New York's Kennedy airport one afternoon. My wife and son were flying home from Illinois. I am not inclined to dwell on morbid thoughts, but for a moment I found myself thinking about the possibility of a crash. What a large part of me would have been destroyed if that plane had gone down. There can be no love without risk.

Christians must be willing to gamble on love. To accept the fact that in loving they are wide open to disappointment and failure. Those we love may let us down.

I believe love today comes into focus most clearly in the racial conflict. Eli Ginsburg, the economist, knows money must be invested if the black man is to be significantly helped. But Ginsburg has decided that far more important than this is a basic change in racial attitudes. "American Negroes need help, but they need acceptance and respect even more," he says.

Ginsburg believes the Negro's main demand is "that racism be exorcised from American life. And only if there is a national commitment to this goal will the many necessary and essential programs of specific assistance to the Negro community have some prospect of succeeding."[4]

Norman Rockwell, the artist, knows personally what Ginsburg is talking about. "Years ago," Rockwell recalls, "a magazine editor told me to never paint a Negro in any position except that of a servant."

Of course there is no way to separate concern from financial commitment. The Bible says that where a man's treasure is, there will his heart be. But our commitment must go further than our wallets. It must reach into our hearts.

Harry Davis is a man whose love goes deep. Davis is a pilot with National Airlines. He has pledged to go wherever necessary to help make a good citizen out of Michael A. Peparo.

Peparo is the twenty-one-year-old youth who held a knife to Davis' back and ordered his jetliner to Cuba last year. Davis, who has four children of his own, says he decided to help the long-haired Peparo minutes after the youth barged into the cockpit with a paring knife in one hand and an insect spray can in the other.

"Initially, I had certain reservations and didn't know

whether he'd use the knife. Then we began discussing the war in Vietnam. His position was that he didn't believe in the draft and didn't want to go over there and kill. He was a very religious boy," said Davis, a veteran of nineteen years with National.

Captain Davis said he and the crew talked Peparo out of going through with the hijacking. Peparo was sent to prison to serve a term for three months to six years. But Captain Davis said, "I will go to this boy wherever he is confined and continue to try to help him. I think he'll be all right now and I think he can be channeled toward becoming a good citizen."

William G. King, Sr., is a man whose love goes deep. King is white. His son, William King, Jr., a U.S. marine, was murdered in Washington, D.C. Three Negroes were charged with the killing. The response of the elder King was to request an integrated honor guard for his son's funeral. He said, "My wife and I feel that the time has come when we have to stand up as individuals . . . for understanding and harmony. Somebody has to make the first step."

King went on to say, "I've been able to wash out of my mind and heart any animosity toward people . . . black or white. I have no desire for revenge."

Dixie Whitted is a woman whose love goes deep. Her husband, Martin, was killed by four teen-agers as he drove his bus through the Hunters Point section of San Francisco. Widowed at the age of thirty, Mrs. Whitted requested that gifts in honor of her slain husband be given to a memorial fund for youth work in Hunters Point. She said, "I want this experience to be a way of helping the minorities of our city."

The widows of Medgar Evers and Martin Luther King, Jr., have demonstrated the depth of their love with the words "We forgive."

Remember that Christian love is measured not by

how much we love those who love us; but rather by how deeply we can feel for those who seem to love us least.

Jesus commanded his followers, "Love your enemies, do good to those who hate you, bless those who curse you, and pray for those who mistreat you." It might help us to understand the implications of this love-ethic if we were to read that command this way: Love the Vietcong. Do good to the Red Chinese. Bless Fidel Castro and Stokely Carmichael and H. Rap Brown. And pray for the leaders in the Kremlin.

Chapter 3

Keepers Are Losers

Only once did Jesus tell of a person going to hell. That person was a rich man who let a beggar starve to death at his front door.

The parable is sometimes cited as an indictment against all wealthy people. I doubt it was intended as such. It is, however, a clear warning that big bank accounts and big hearts don't necessarily share the same owner.

It is sad to see a man mastered by money. It is reported that when P. T. Barnum died, his very last words were a request to see the day's circus receipts.

Now there's nothing inherently wrong with money. It can build a hospital, staff a school, or put food in empty stomachs. But money is dangerous, for it has almost mystical powers to bring out the worst in a man.

Dr. Norman V. Hope says that learning how to handle prosperity has been a difficult task for Christians in every age. He adds that the problem "has never been more acute than it is in American society today."'[1]

Then Hope outlines some of the pitfalls of affluence: First, there's the temptation to figure we made it on our own; that our wealth is nothing more than a just reward for initiative, ingenuity, and hard work. Well, that may be partly true. But Dr. Hope believes such an attitude lacks both gratitude and humility. It fails to recognize the help others handed us as we climbed the success-ladder. It fails to acknowledge those quirks of fate—those happy accidents—which contributed to our prosperity. And above all, such an attitude fails to take into account opportunities and talents which, through no effort on our part, were uniquely ours.

Then there's the temptation to consider wealth God's gift to those of superior virtue. That view certainly doesn't square with the Bible, nor will it stand up under the scrutiny of our own experiences. The most virtuous man who ever lived was rewarded, not with blue chip stocks, but with a brutal cross. During his final meal with his followers, Jesus predicted that they, too, would suffer if they were true to him.

It is easy for those of us who have it made to say of those who don't, "They're just lazy. They could make it, too, if they'd go to work." It's easy to say, but is it true?

Not according to the latest and the best evidence collected by social scientists and other experts in the field of hard-core poverty. They've found that a majority of the chronically poor in America begin their lives in a straitjacket of handicaps most can never escape without help.

The cycle of failure is easy enough to define, but agonizingly difficult to break: poor family, poor education, poor job, poor family. It's fine to encourage people to pull themselves up by their own bootstraps; but some people have no bootstraps.

It is easy for us to stand at the altar of abundance and, in a loud voice, thank God that we are not as other men. Jesus denounced such attitudes. He warned us against that kind of self-righteousness. He declared that rich men would have a tough time getting into the kingdom. Not because money is bad, but because it can do bad things to people.

Americans are the wealthiest people in the world. Families with modest incomes enjoy luxuries ancient kings didn't even dream about. But not all American families have even modest incomes. While the rich get richer, the poor too often get platitudes. Now, morally sensitive people are beginning to ask some morally embarrassing questions.

For instance, how can a nation with a gross national product of nearly $900 billion permit millions of its citizens to go hungry?

The evidence has been trickling down on the Christian conscience for a long time. Now, it has become an avalanche. A senate investigating committee recently added convincing statistics, indicating a much larger malnutrition problem in the United States than even most critics had believed. The reports show millions of children exist on inadequate diets—diets so lacking in basic essentials that minds and bodies are hopelessly stunted before the children ever reach school age.

The reports show that for poor whites in Appalachia, for black Americans in city ghettos and rural areas, for Spanish Americans and Indians and Eskimos and migrant farm workers, hunger is an everyday circumstance.

Men and women of Christian conscience may honestly differ over the campus crisis, the antiballistic missile system, the federal budget, or the income surtax. But hunger is a clear-cut issue. The very cornerstone of Christian commitment is compassion. We can hardly call ourselves Christ's followers if we are indifferent to hungry children—whether in Biafra or in Baltimore.

It should be clear that the responsibility for sharing the loaves and fishes has passed into our hands. If people starve, it is not because of God's will—but because we lack goodwill.

The gap which separates rich and poor is widening, not only between individuals but between nations. Just as failure to narrow that gap here in the United States has invited open violence, so failure to narrow that gap in the world is an invitation to war.

Secretary General U Thant of the United Nations warns of what he calls a "prosperous provincialism" in international life. He says poor countries are increasingly impatient at the denial of adequate help for them to bridge the gap. During a summer session of the U.N. Economic and Social Council in Geneva, U Thant warned the rich nations that "their future prosperity and security and that of their children and grandchildren is inextricably linked with the well-being of people in the developing countries."[2]

U Thant was simply saying that self-interest compels modern man to be concerned for the welfare of others. It's not really a new idea. Jesus expressed it when he said a man has to lose himself to save himself. The person who tries too hard to save will lose.

This principle is confirmed in science, in history, and in our personal experience. The Bible states it several times, in different ways: "Cast your bread upon the waters, for you will find it after many days" (Ecc. 11:1, RSV). "Every one who has left houses or brothers or sisters or father or mother or children or fields for my sake, will receive a hundred times more" (Matt. 19:29, TEV). "Many who now are first will be last, and many who now are last will be first" (v. 30). "Do for others what you want them to do for you" (Matt. 7:12,

TEV). "It is more blessed to give than to receive" (Acts 20:35, RSV).

However phrased, the meaning is clear: *keepers are losers.* It is a law of life—a statutory law, written throughout the Bible; a common law of nature with precedent in every generation.

I am personally acquainted with men who have amassed vast fortunes and in the process lost their sense of values, their sensitivity to others, their friends, and in some cases, their families and their health. Not all wealthy men have paid such terrible prices for financial success, but many have. Those who cling tightly to monetary empires rather than use those resources as channels of creativeness and concern end up as losers and weepers.

I recall writing a news account of a man found dead in the tiny shack he occupied near a dump. Everyone supposed he had been a pauper. But inside his hovel was discovered nearly $100,000 in cash. It was stuffed under the ragged mattress, hidden in broken drawers, slipped beneath cracked linoleum. Here was a man whose warped sense of values had enslaved him to the god of capital—a man so possessed by his possessions, he refused even to buy for himself the things he obviously needed.

There are other true stories like that, for the god of greed is a ferocious deity—never satisfied, never appeased.

Projected onto an international scale, this law that *keepers are losers* has profound implications. U Thant spelled out one of them when he warned that unshared affluence is an open invitation to violence.

Observe, now, another warning—this one from Dr. Pierre-Marie Dorolle, Deputy Director-General of the World Health Organization.[3] Dr. Dorolle notes that poor nations always have been reservoirs of disease—

the kinds of disease which cause epidemics. Now, the jet-age has added new dangers to the old plagues. A passenger infected in Africa, for instance, can be in Asia or Europe or the United States within a matter of hours.

Supersonic planes soon will be rocketing people from one continent to another at 1,500 miles per hour, or more. That means dreaded diseases will be able to cross the oceans just that much faster.

Dorolle points out that in the past twenty-two years, some eighty cases of smallpox in western countries have been traced to Africa, South America, and Asia. One case entering the U.S. in 1947 led to twelve secondary cases with two deaths and the expenditure of thousands of dollars to vaccinate six million New Yorkers. Dr. Dorolle concludes that in this fast-moving world, the only way to prevent the old plagues—and some new ones—from spreading, is for the wealthy nations to help the poorest nations reach such a level of economic and technical development that they will be able to combat such diseases at the source.

Modern transportation has, indeed, shrunk our entire world into a neighborhood. While we don't yet seem willing to create of this neighborhood a brotherhood, it is in our own self-interest to share our medical and scientific abundance with the less fortunate.

Self-interest, of course, is the lowest form of motivation for doing what is morally right. Jesus taught not only service to strangers, but love for enemies. In fact, his emphasis was upon attitude. Undoubtedly, the world would be better if we did what was right; but it would be best of all if we did what was right for the right reasons.

I remember reading a New Year's resolution which went something like this: "I will try at least once each day to offer an unexpected compliment to someone who can't possibly do me any good."

How refreshing to encounter people who do good without an angle. Such people are the real winners in the world. Their trophies include self-respect, sense of purpose, peace of mind—qualities the poorest among us can have, but the richest among us cannot buy.

Byron Frederick says the world is composed of takers and givers. The *takers* eat better. But the *givers* sleep better.[4]

There is encouraging evidence that many Americans, especially young people, are beginning to discover this ancient and inviolable truth: *Keepers are losers*. Or, to state it in the positive: *Givers are winners!*

During a recent visit to the United States, Ian Waller of London's Sunday Telegraph said he found much that is hopeful in America. "I have talked to scores of people, black and white, all over the country, who are working on race relations committees, the poverty programs, urban development and education integration schemes. The dedication, sincerity and effort is very moving."[5]

Sharing material wealth is only one form of helping. It is an important part of giving, but there are others equally as important. No amount of money can staff a hospital with well-trained doctors and nurses if there are no well-trained doctors and nurses. Contributions to seminaries, no matter how substantial, cannot produce ministers unless there are students to attend those seminaries.

Giving involves wallets, but it involves much more. It involves people. Perhaps there is a greater desire for self-giving than most of us believe. For instance, I think much of what we label apathy could more accurately be described as ignorance. To be sure, there are indifferent and uncaring individuals. There are people whose consciences have not been sparked by this dynamic love-concept.

But, in the words of one Roman Catholic priest in Biafra: "Everyone wants to help Biafra . . . the trouble is, they don't know how."

I submit this is part of our problem in the United States. There must be millions of Americans who sincerely want to do something about the critical problems of our day, but who don't know how. They see no clear avenues for direct service. They haven't found handles for their concern.

Many are asking, "What can I do in an immediate, personal way to reach the slum child? The teen-ager who's in trouble? The inner-city family which happens to have a culture or color different from mine?"

I *sense* more goodwill among us than I *see*. I know that whenever avenues for service open, people respond.

When the Peace Corps was first established, skeptics said it would never work. The Corps promised America's most gifted young people only one reward: a chance to serve. In return for their talents, toil, sweat, and aching muscles, the volunteers were to receive less than the legal minimum wage. Less than a part-time sacker in a supermarket could make after school.

The Peace Corps demanded long hours, hard work, and sacrifice. But the skeptics had overlooked the idealism which had long been cultivated in the minds of American youth. Peace Corps offices were flooded with applications—far more than they could process.

A similar kind of challenge attracted people to Jesus. He offered his young disciples no life of ease, but they gave up everything to follow him. He promised hardship and predicted death, but they left family, friends, and vocations to answer his call. They gave up the good life to follow his good way of life the way of service;

the way of sharing; the way of concern; the way of the cross.

Young people still respond to such a challenge, often with a depth of commitment which shocks their elders. It is a disservice to offer today's youth security when they long for commitment.

Consider the case of Glen Chedester, a conscientious objector from Walla Walla, Washington.[7] Glen came out of Vietnam a decorated war hero; yet during his entire year there, he never fired a shot—never carried a gun.

Glen Chedester was twenty-one when he went to Vietnam as an army medic. He says some of the guys figured he was a coward, or crazy, not to carry a gun. All that changed on April 12, 1968. It happened to be Good Friday. It also was the day Vietcong forces broke through the outer defenses around Glen's camp.

He doesn't remember all the details of that predawn battle. He does remember fleeting glimpses of enemy troops, the distinct impression that somebody was trying to kill him, and a lot of men yelling for a medic.

Glen Chedester, treating fifteen or sixteen men in less than three hours, dodged bullets and defied death to pull the wounded to safety. This young medic, armed only with his faith in God, his commitment to others, and a small medical kit, won the Distinguished Service Cross. That's the nation's second highest medal for bravery. But Glen Chedester, who believes it's wrong to kill, won a lot more than that.

Another giver who's gaining is Dr. Leonard Linde of Los Angeles.[8] In 1967, Dr. Linde organized a group called the Committee of Responsibility. Quietly, and with little fanfare, this group started bringing Vietnamese children to the United States for medical treatment, children badly maimed by bullets or napalm. All of them are children whose bodies need rebuilding.

The little victims are given the best care America can provide. They are treated in the best hospitals and medical centers. According to Dr. Linde, it costs from $5,000 to $10,000 to treat each child, but the committee believes it's worth the money and the effort.

Some skeptics claim Dr. Linde's program is mere tokenism, that it can't begin to cope with the enormous problem of child war victims in Vietnam. That is true. But no man is justified in doing nothing simply because he can't do everything. Linde says if his committee helps save only one life, the project will be worthwhile.

These are not isolated instances. Almost daily news stories cross my desk telling of some sacrifice, some personal commitment somebody has made for others. Occasionally the story is dramatic: like the one about the Canadian social worker who chained himself to a bed in a leper's hospital in Ceylon. He wanted to protest the social stigma associated with the dreaded disease, and to identify with its victims.

But there is a lot of undramatic, unpublicized giving and sharing going on in our world: Like those wealthy suburbanites in several communities around Washington, D.C., who have started having ghetto children as summer guests, to share their swimming pools and their patios.

Like the thousand teen-agers who marched twenty-five miles from Port Jefferson to East Northport, New York, to raise money for starving Biafrans. They stopped drivers along the way and collected $10,000.

Like Dick Kraus, a prisoner at the Colorado State Penitentiary, who donated thirty dollars from his prison earnings so a needy family in Canon City could have a Thanksgiving Day dinner. Most of that thirty dollars Kraus had earned at the rate of twenty-five cents a day.

Like Lockheed aircraft, a company that's launched a

program to hire and train men with prison records. Now, other companies are doing it, too.

Like the folks in Hartford, Connecticut, who founded a Revitalization Corps, a kind of private Peace Corps for adults who want to increase human understanding through direct, face-to-face contact with the needy. This program builds bridges of concern between suburbs and ghettos in several states.

In his inaugural address, President Nixon spoke of "legions of the concerned and committed" who by "small, splendid efforts" can "build a great cathedral of the spirit." Perhaps in time, there will be legions of caring, sharing people. But we are now only at the platoon or squad level. It may be many years before our small, splendid efforts produce anything resembling a great cathedral of the spirit.

Still, as the late Senator Robert Kennedy once observed, each committed life sends out ripples, like a pebble dropped into the water. Perhaps, in time, these ripples will merge into a mighty tide of compassion. When that happens, mankind will be the winner.

Chapter 4

Fun City

Henry Vollam Morton could have been thinking of New York when he wrote those words, "in the hideous roar of a city . . ."! New York—with its unbearable noise, unbreathable air, unlivable tenements, immovable traffic, inevitable strikes. New York—a myriad of seemingly unsolvable problems.

Mayor John Lindsay once dubbed this incredible town Fun City. New Yorkers have been laughing ever since.

I suppose New York, as cities go, has about as much fun in it as any other place with too many people and too little land; too much competition and too little compassion; too much lust and too little love; too much greed and too little gratitude.

New York, of course, has no exclusive claim on these dubious distinctions. So enormous are the problems of all America's industrial centers that a whole new vocabulary has evolved. It includes phrases such as "the urban crisis," "city in turmoil," "concrete jungle," "flight to the suburbs," "crisis of environment." Each phrase calls to mind critical circumstances which are anything but funny.

Our comedians still make jokes about the rising crime rates, increase in drug abuse, understaffed and overburdened welfare systems, air and water pollution, traffic congestion, and noise. We laugh. But deep down inside, we know the joke is on us, for these are our cities. These are our crises.

Several times since moving to New York, I have thought about the biblical account of Jesus standing on a hillside, looking down at Jerusalem and weeping. Can we comprehend the grief he might show were he to stand atop the Palisades today and look down on New York City? Or make a helicopter inspection tour of Chicago? Or walk through Los Angeles? Pittsburgh? or Boston?

Much lesser men have had their hearts broken as they surveyed the tragedy of Watts, the misery of Harlem, the distress and despair of Newark.

I can never forget my visit to Newark. It was on a long, hot night in July 1967. That steaming, urban jungle—just across the river from New York City—had exploded in violence. ABC had sent me to cover what history would record as The Newark Riots.

I remember lying flat on the sticky pavement of Springfield Avenue as police and sniper bullets whined overhead. For nearly twenty minutes we were pinned down by the continuous blaze of gunfire.

That night, I saw a fireman shot in the face. I watched him die.

I talked with a young girl whose mother was killed by a police bullet while she watched television inside their tenement.

I saw anger and alienation in the eyes of young blacks; anguish and despair in the eyes of the old; fear and distrust in the faces of children.

I remember the eyes of policemen and national guardsmen. Eyes which transmitted a discordant symphony of emotions, from frustration to hatred. There was little evidence of compassion or understanding on either side of that black-white line—that line which runs between the aggrieved and the achieved, between the oppressed minority and the often insensitive majority.

I prayed for Newark that night. I saw some pretty tough guys—police-beat reporters, hard-nosed city hall types—get lumps in their throats as they gazed into the decaying entrails of a ghetto. Some of them looked as though they might be praying, too.

I do not remember the exact words, but I was thinking, *Father, forgive them. They don't know what they're doing. Forgive the looter. Forgive the sniper. Forgive the trigger-happy policeman. Forgive the frightened, inexperienced guardsman whose shouted insult to a Negro woman may have resulted more from fear than from racism. Forgive all these creatures who are hating each other tonight. Forgive all of us for not having cared enough.*

After the last shot was fired, the last window broken, the last corpse carried off to the morgue, it was all over for me. Newark was to become just a memory, as I returned to my comfortable home in the all-white, all-right, part of my city.

It was not over for them. For them, the nightmare would live on. No one who'd been there could think of Newark as fun city.

Of course, if you can afford it, the city—any city—provides as many pleasant distractions as it does problems.

Surround yourself with the blast and blare of a downtown discotheque and you'll hardly hear the soft cries of loneliness outside.

Seat yourself comfortably on the aisle of a rollicking Broadway musical and you'll seldom think about rats running up and down the halls of Harlem's dingy and dilapidated dwellings.

Take yourself out to the ball game. It's a lot more fun watching the Yankees or the Mets on the lush lawn of a manicured park than to think of hapless kids playing kick the can in some litter strewn alley. Dining at "21" sure beats worrying about school dropouts, teen-aged dope addicts, or hungry babies.

More than a hundred years ago, Charles Dickens began his *A Tale of Two Cities* with the line, "It was the best of times, it was the worst of times." Today, every major metropolis in America is two cities. For some, it is the best of times. For others, it is hell.

There are now more than 200 million people in the United States. At the present growth rate, there could be more than 400 million within fifty years. Much of the growth will occur in the cities. At the beginning of the twentieth century well over half the population lived on farms or in small towns. Today 70 percent live in and around the big cities.

Peter Drucker says: "Within a few years three quarters of the American people will live in a fairly small number of metropolitan areas . . . fewer than 200. And nearly two-fifths of the population will live in or close by three, monster super-cities."[1]

Frightening, isn't it? Stack those statistics up against the present, pressing needs for decent housing, adequate schools, transportation, cleaner environment, and a better quality of life, and the projection is overwhelming.

Such forecasts may explain why Stephanie Mill of Phoenix made the kind of speech she did at her commencement last spring. Stephanie is a pretty, twenty-year-old coed, who was valedictorian of her class at Mills College in Oakland, California. In her valedictory speech, Stephanie shocked the audience by announcing she had decided never to have children.

She said, "The most humane thing for me to do is to have no children at all. Mankind has horribly disfigured this planet. As an ex-potential parent I have asked myself what kind of world my children would grow up in. And the answer is not very pretty. Not very clean. Sad in fact."[2]

As the father of a young son, I share Stephanie's concern. No, much more than concern. Alarm—for time does not appear to be on our side.

The crisis of the cities is a challenge to the committed. I hope—I even suspect—that the Christian community may be on the threshold of a positive, massive response. I sense a growing concern for the cities in church conferences I attend. I hear it in my conversations with church laymen. I see it in literature now being published by the church. There seems to be a new militancy among believers. It can be heard in the singing of hymns. Sometimes it comes from the pulpit. Perhaps this slumbering giant we call the church is once again about to live up to its great commission.

Don't get me wrong. I am not at all sure the institutionalized church will be able to keep pace with the renewal that seems to be igniting much of the membership. Perhaps the church organization is too encumbered by archaic machinery; too overweight with peripheral programs and secondary objectives. Maybe those structures we sometimes mistake for the church will remain wrapped in ecclesiastical insulation, out of contact with the real world.

But the real church—that coalition of the concerned—seems more than ever to be moving out toward the cutting edge of life.

Remember, the first church had no building, no prayer books, not even an altar or a creed. It was simply a group of men who were friends of Jesus. Men who believed what he said about loving people and about turning the other cheek. They had differing points of view about a lot of matters. But they all seemed to know that it's more important to care than to agree.

I am discovering among my friends—Catholic, Jewish, and Protestant—an increased moral sensitivity, coupled with a tacit acknowledgement that man's institutions are not doing the job. They have promised better than they have performed.

I sense, especially among the thinking young, an awareness that man's ultimate hope is a spiritual hope; that the problem of the cities, like the problem of war, is essentially a human problem. Essentially, it too will require an adequate answer to the human dilemma.

The SDS (Students for a Democratic Society) tells us our cities can be saved only through revolution. I agree. But their revolution is inadequate. They simply want to change the system. Surely, some parts of the system ought to be changed. But rearranging, overhauling, or even destroying government machinery won't cure our sick cities; for the source of the disease is man himself.

What our cities require is a moral revolution, the kind Jesus preached. His was, after all, the first really revolutionary concept to come along in centuries. Long before his birth men had dreamed of Utopia. Many thinkers had pondered the possibility of social change—of restructuring society.

Jesus went far beyond that. He did not deny the need for social change. He endorsed it. But Jesus said man can change—man's nature can change: Love can replace hate. Generosity can overcome greed. Jesus' great society was to be built with new men, not merely new conditions.

Some still argue whether he came to save individuals or to save society. It is a senseless argument, for the two objectives are inseparable. Jesus clearly came to revolutionize individual men *and* to revolutionize their way of relating to each other.

There would be little logic in debating whether medicine is responsible for the health of individuals rather than for the health of the nation. How can the two be contradictory? They are complementary.

Of course the medical profession is concerned with healing individuals. But when certain problems, such as cigarette smoking or air pollution, endanger sufficient numbers of people, we then speak of a *national* health problem. Mass inoculations, city-wide health campaigns, national drives against disease, are never thought of as conflicting with medicine's responsibility to the individual.

So it is that Christianity, to be relevant in this age, must speak not only to the soul and intellect of individual men, but to the great social issues of the day as well.

The question is not whether the church will take a stand on such matters as poverty, racial equality, equal employment, decent housing, and war. Dr. John Coventry Smith says that refusing to take a stand is—in itself

—taking a stand. Silence can give consent and there are some issues of such moral magnitude that a relevant church cannot keep silent.

There is no denying that some church groups, some local congregations, some individual church members are dragging their feet on these crucial controversies. But many are putting themselves where the action is; and so much of the action today is in the cities.

People are drawn closer together in times of trouble. In city after city, I have seen people of differing backgrounds and persuasions pull together when confronted with a common crisis. I witnessed such a spirit of *community unity* during New York City's big power blackout in 1965.

I have reported launches from Cape Kennedy since the early days of manned space flight, and I'm always impressed by the way the entire space center becomes as one man on launch day. The word *team* is insufficient to describe the spirit of common purpose which seems to captivate everyone—technicians, newsmen, even the people who operate the stores and restaurants at Cocoa Beach. As the countdown clock ticks toward lift-off, every man, woman, and child around the Cape appears possessed by a single compulsion to get the astronauts on their way—safely.

Perhaps the genuinely committed are showing the way. Many a Methodist minister, Catholic priest, and Jewish rabbi has marched arm-in-arm against war or racial injustice. Could it be we are witnessing the first signs of crisis cooperation at the spiritual level?

Maybe we are finally developing the thrust necessary to launch a meaningful campaign of concern for man himself. Maybe we are finally recognizing that great spiritual goals—like great space goals—cannot be attained on a narrow, partisan, parochial basis. All men of good will must pool their knowledge and their dedicated efforts. Rivalries and suspicions must give way to mutual respect and trust.

I sometimes think it would be easier for the older generation to pass through the eye of a needle than to shed its religious prejudices; but, fortunately, many kids seem to be shedding theirs. Perhaps you didn't hear the story about a Christmas message Jewish teen-agers in Chicago sent to their Christian brothers.[3] The story probably was crowded out of your newspaper by accounts of campus riots, teen-age drug abuse, or hippies. It was not a sensational story, but it was a significant one, for it spoke volumes about the moral sensitivities of modern youth.

The message began, "In times like these we must stop and commit our lives to change and improve the world in which we live." It went on to stress the need for combating "apathy in the secular age which seems to have subordinated moral standards and spiraled the world into an orbit of indifference towards man and his problems."

That Christmas greeting from the young Jews to the young Christians noted the "times of war" and the "misguided passions of men." It called for a joining of Christian and Jew during the "reflective holiday period" to start working today—not tomorrow—toward the goals of seeking a newer world. The message went on to state:

We are growing up in a world where our parents have succumbed to the secular age and the crass commercial value systems in our society negate moral codes. This indifference applies to religion, where we learn the message of human compassions. Religion has lost a great deal of our commitment due to its double standards between preachment and action.

Then, the message issued a call for joint action: "As we assume the leaderships in our faith groups, we must make certain that we do not repeat the same errors. Together, we must restore in daily practice the basic tenets of religion."

Reading that thoughtful greeting suggests that we, perhaps, too easily indict our young for alleged godlessness. They may, indeed, be marching to the beat of different drums. But they just may make theirs one of the most morally sensitive and spirtually attuned generations yet born. It undoubtedly is their acute awareness which causes some of their hang-ups about organized religion.

For one thing, many youngsters today find it much more difficult than we to wink at gaps of credibility. They somehow have the idea that performance should bear some resemblance to profession. They seem to think a person who proclaims the fatherhood of God and brotherhood of man ought to practice such proclamations in his daily life. They obviously feel that a nation which preaches "liberty and justice for all" should actually extend those rights to every person.

Remember Eliza Doolittle's rage in "My Fair Lady" when she declared, "Words, words, I'm so sick of words. If you're in love, show me." It is a hopeful sign that so many young people today are demanding deeds, not discourse.

We should not forget that young people played a more active role in the 1968 presidential election than in any previous campaign in United States history. One candidate's campaign became known as the "children's crusade" and he referred to himself as a sort of pied piper. Youthful idealism was a potent if not decisive force in that election. Give kids a cause, a red-hot issue, a significant reason for activism, and the response can be awesome.

The new generation is not interested in the old standards of negative righteousness. They find the tedious task of itemizing activities into acceptable and unacceptable categories a totally inadequate approach to life. They're calling the bluff on those pharisaical Christians who read them the riot act on marijuana smoking, then vote to keep Negroes out of their neighborhoods. They're challenging both the logic and the sincerity of those pseudosaints who quote the parable of the good Samaritan, then pass by *on the other side* as apathy and prejudice rob their fellowmen and beat them into the unconsciousness of despair.

Young people today seem little inspired by churchmen who try to mask their social indifference with shields of personal piety. They have even less respect for a church which condones, even sanctions, such a superficial approach to evil.

These kids are most certainly concerned with the problem of evil. Dr. Theodore Hesburgh says of today's college students: "They are more informed, more widely read, better educated, more idealistic and more deeply sensitive to crucial moral issues in our times—more likely to dedicate themselves to good rather than selfish goals than any past generation of students I have known."[4]

Dean James Ault, of Drew University Theological School, says the ministerial students he meets impress him as being persons of integrity and intelligence and no small amount of political wisdom. "Their desire to minister is clear. There is a sense of commitment to the ministry and to the church, but not necessarily to the church as it now is."[5]

When the British parliament several years ago was considering a revision of the prayerbook, one member reportedly stood during the debate and said, "For God's sake, don't touch the Church of England. It's the only thing that stand between us and Christianity."

It's true but sad that the institutional church—with

its symbols, its rituals, its assurances—often protects people from the legitimate claims of Christ. Shakespeare might well have been describing a church which has lost its mission when he wrote, "Lilies that fester smell far worse than weeds."

It is not Christianity, but perversions and distortions of it, that many young people are rejecting. They are repelled, not by the pure teachings of the gospel, but by the pollution of that gospel and the stench of hypocrisy.

Some critics, both inside and outside the church, insist the church is not—and cannot be—adequate to the challenge of the cities. I must dissent from that view—for if there is no hope for a spiritual solution, then there is no hope for any solution.

Concrete and steel, factories and school buildings, roads and apartments—these can only change man's environment. They cannot change man. Our cities are in desperate need of urban renewal, but they just as desperately need human renewal. These are not separate problems but part of the same problem.

Into these centers of crisis and frustration, the church is challenged to carry her holy optimism; her visionary ability to see more than there is in everything; her creative ability to convert the desirable into the actual.

The church cannot save the cities if it insists on being an island—a sort of fallout shelter against the turmoil of our time. It must not mimic the fundamentalist Bible college I read about recently. That school has a high fence around its campus, locked and guarded at night. Security is so tight an intelligent thought probably would have difficulty infiltrating the campus. Recently the school administration asked state permission to arm its guards with submachine guns and automatic rifles, claiming this would be a precaution against trouble on campus. The state had the good judgment to say No. I realize Jesus promised that the gates of hell would not prevail against his church; but, I doubt that he meant for his promise to be backed up by bullets.

Nearly 600 years before Jesus was born, Alcaeus observed, "Not houses . . . make the city, but men able to use their opportunity."

George MacLeod recognizes the relevance of Jesus' teachings to the sick, sad, sprawling metropolis. He urges that the

> . . . cross be raised again at the center of the market-place as well as on the steeple of the church. I am recovering the claim that Jesus was not crucified in a cathedral between two candles, but on a cross between two thieves; on the town garbage heap; at a crossroad so cosmopolitan that they had to write his title in Hebrew and in Latin and in Greek . . . at the kind of place where cynics talk smut, and thieves curse, and soldiers gamble. Because that is where he died. And that is what he died about. And that is where churchmen ought to be, and what churchmen ought to be about.[6]

The Christian view recognizes that cities are both houses and men, places and people, environment and inhabitants. When we see the city like it is, and when we see the gospel like it is, we know they were meant for each other.

Chapter 5

A Cool Cat

Harry Truman once counseled that a President who didn't like the heat should get out of the kitchen. That's not bad advice, except now the heat is on everybody; and, there is no way to get out.

Space travel may someday open up new frontiers for a few venturesome souls who want to rocket out of this world and start over on another planet. In the meantime, earth is the only home we have. We must make the best of it.

One of the most telling titles to flash across a Broadway marquee was "Stop the World, I Want to Get Off." Who hasn't felt that way at one time or another?

But, the world doesn't stop. It seems to whirl at an ever more maddening pace; pressures build, tensions increase, the heat rises, and modern man's mental and emotional endurance at times are strained past the breaking point.

Stress has become synonymous with life in this twentieth century. Some sociologists and psychologists believe much of the violence we have today is simply stress, carried to its logical but tragic conclusion. They see some assault, rioting, and killing, as emotional escape valves.

Louis Cassels recently outlined the typical tensions a city dweller may encounter on an average working day:

> He is aroused from too-little sleep by the strident jangling of an alarm clock. As he gulps a hasty breakfast, he glances over the front page of a newspaper, and finds most of the news disturbing. He hurries out to catch his commuter bus, but finds it already full so he has to stand, wedged into a sweaty mass of humanity, while the bus lumbers into town through bumper-to-bumper, rush-hour traffic. At the office, he tries to get some work done despite interruptions by the telephone, "drop everything" summonses from higher authority, and other aggravations.
>
> It's a rare day when at least one person—boss, subordinate, client or office boy—fails to do or say something that angers him. By quitting time, his stomach's likely to be all tied in knots. Whatever good humor he had left evaporates on the return bus ride, and he arrives at home ready to growl at his wife with the slightest provocation.
>
> His wife, meanwhile, has also had a frustrating day—trying to get a plumber to come fix a leaky pipe, fighting a telephone battle with a department store that made a mistake in her bill, and prying the children away from the television set long enough to make a pass at their homework. She's in no mood to serve as a lightning rod for her husband's accumulated hostilities.[1]

Cassels doubts this is an exaggerated picture. And he reminds us that this is the picture of a lucky American—one who has a home in the suburbs and a white-collar job. Consider how much greater are the stresses on those who live in overcrowded ghettos, and have no meaningful jobs.

Malcolm Boyd's perceptive prayer book, *Are You Running With Me, Jesus?*, mirrors both the challenge and the confusion which surround the modern Christian. Boyd's down-to-earth—and earthy—conversations with God reflect a strong conviction that Jesus is relevant to the era of young-looking skin, lite-diet desserts, and perma-press shirts. Boyd, obviously, is not ready to throw in the spiritual sponge and say last rites for the Christian faith. He recognizes that a hostile environment can toughen the Christian, just as it did those first followers of Jesus who had to meet secretly in caves, and who faced death if they were discovered.

Too many fainthearts today would say to the church what a new army lieutenant said to his troops. It was the young officer's first time to lead a march since receiving his commission. He thought he knew all the commands. But when his men came to a high fence, the lieutenant couldn't remember a single order for getting his men across. So, he improvised: "Company halt! Disband and reassemble on the other side!" There are those who would have the church simply liquidate and, perhaps, reassemble at some future time when the conditions would be more favorable.

The fact is, the church has its biggest job to do when the conditions of life are least favorable. At least one writer has described courage as grace under pressure! A real Christian is not a pious, long-faced mystic who shuts himself behind cloistered walls to read a prayer book. He is much more apt to be found fighting a traffic jam, dictating an interoffice memo, nailing a rafter in place, or debating a proposed city ordinance at a local council meeting.

The committed person needs time to meditate, to think about life, to quietly communicate with God and with his own inner being. But the Christian is not looking for escape. He seeks encounter and conflict in the real world of action. Not as some caped crusader, but as a concerned human being. Not as one who considers himself better than anybody else, but as a person who wants to help make life better for everybody. Real Christians have, traditionally, turned their backs on the comfort and tranquility of the temple and moved into the streets of combat and transition. A real Christian is a cool cat, who willingly walks into the heat of conflict.

Jesus did proclaim inner peace to individuals, but it was not peace at any price. Babies in the womb are at peace. People who remain intellectually and spiritually in the womb of unawareness are at peace; but it is peace purchased at the expense of reality.

If the world is a tempest, then the Christian wants to be battling the waves; not moored at the dock, or sitting out the storms from the comfort of the shore. Whatever is out there, he wants to experience it. The Christian wants the fullest possible awareness of this mysterious journey called life.

Such passion for adventure may mark the Christian as some sort of nut. An oddball. A crackpot. In a sense, there is something, at least *unusual,* about anyone today who believes in a cause enough to work for it and, if necessary, to die for it. A Christian, motivated as he ought to be by concern for others, may seem strange in this superambitious society where everyone seems to claw for advantage. Yet, what better way to carry out Christ's commandments than to bring his spirit of love and humility into the competition of the marketplace?

In this day when pleasure is the supreme principle, when expediency replaces ethics, when those with convictions are sometimes considered square, perhaps following Jesus' way simply means showing a better way. The world needs to see transformed lives.

But don't expect a medal for taking the high road. When you insist on making it harder on yourself than you have to, simply because it's right, you tend to stand out. When you insist on taking life seriously, you seem different. When you go against the group for no better reason than an ethical motivation, a lot of people won't understand. Your refusal to take it easy and roll with the punches may cause some to question your maturity and judgment.

Nor will everyone understand the persistent optimism of a Christ-centered life. This doesn't mean Christians never suffer depression—never have the blues. But there is a constant undercurrent of happiness which flows from a vital faith. Some will misconstrue, others will mistrust it.

Russell Baker was at his best when he wrote a satirical piece, "The Public Enemy."[2] The column fictitiously describes what happens in Manhattan when a man wakes up feeling good one beautiful May morning. There's no special reason, no logic to it. This man simply wakes up with a song in his throat and a smile on his face. Baker then describes how this pleasant chap becomes suspect; how alarms sound throughout the city, warning the pessimistic populace that some screwball is walking around without his gloom and guilt. As the unusual man happily makes his way through the corridors and streets of the city, his personal sense of well-being creates first resentment, then panic. Finally, the man is branded a public enemy—criminal.

Perhaps only a crackpot would dare to walk with confidence through such an era as ours. Who but a dunce could remain cool and poised in this nuclear-fused and politically confused world? Maybe this is what the Apostle Paul had in mind when he referred to himself as a fool for Christ.

So let's once and for all knock off the notion that a person who commits himself to Jesus' way will automatically earn the love and respect of his contemporaries. Anyone who sincerely tries to love his enemies may be regarded as gullible. Anyone who sincerely attempts to befriend those who mistreat him may be branded a rube. Anyone who insists on turning the other cheek may get it slugged. This should not be surprising. It is precisely what Jesus predicted.

Somewhere along the way, we got our theology twisted. We began to think of Christianity as simply another name for respectability. We started equating commitment with esteem. A Christian won't always come off looking like a jolly good guy. Sometimes he has to oppose his peers; go against the group. He should not be shocked if such behavior fails to increase his popularity.

Genuine commitment can be guaranteed to make people uncomfortable. It is disconcerting to be around someone whose motives seem higher, purer than one's own. It is humiliating to have one's dark and tawdry life laid bare by the brilliance of another's idealism. Throughout history, lesser men have sought to destroy —to extinguish—such lights. The moral midgets of Jesus' day were determined to cut this spiritual superman down to their size. When they could not, they conspired to kill him. Those who have taken seriously his challenges have been risking death ever since.

There are many ways to *kill* a man. The modern believer in America usually doesn't face physical death, although a string of recent assassinations makes the safety of committed men a matter of growing concern. The contemporary Christian does confront the very real possibility of character assassination. And sometimes, words can be mightier than the sword.

I have heard the motives of truly honorable men questioned by those who contend no man can act unselfishly. It seems to be a sign of sophistication to debunk great aims and lofty purposes. Perhaps the motto is, "If you can't join 'em, lick 'em." If you can't match their nobility, then deny it or depreciate it. But never, never admit that a man can be genuinely generous. To admit that possibility is to set a similar standard for yourself.

There is no verbal argument sufficient to counter the

charge, "Everybody's got an angle." But I see that accusation being refuted every day in dozens of small, and sometimes large, ways. I see people demonstrating authentic decency in their routine encounters. I know people who, unquestionably, are motivated by compassion and love.

Well, the job of living a committed life in such a cynical age can be very rewarding for anyone with the stomach—and the heart—for it. Some tough and arduous work has been assigned this generation. I remember seeing a circle of barricades around a small area of Fifth Avenue in New York City one day. Posted signs warned, Danger—Men Working. It occurred to me that danger is always present where men are working. Anyone who tries to do something constructive faces risks if no more than the risk of unfair censure. A Christian—in this day—has to be a cool cat.

My job as a newsman is to tell people what's happening. More than that, it is to make them think about what's happening. Troubling people's minds is almost as dangerous as disturbing their consciences.

On a flight from Cape Kennedy to New York one morning, I sat next to David Brinkley. Discussing our role as newsmen, we agreed that most people are personally upset by bad news. They don't like it. Furthermore, we agreed that a lot of people resent those who have to present the unfortunate and unpleasant truth. David told me he had received thousands of letters protesting the way radio and television covered the demonstrations in Chicago during the 1968 Democratic convention. He was obviously disturbed by this massive, negative reaction. The famous Brinkley grin was gone as he said, "You know, Mort, I'm convinced people really don't want us to tell it like it is."

He was right. Too many people would rather remain serene in their illusions than to face facts. This is why prophets and preachers in every age have been prime targets of anger, even violence. They are most vulnerable when they are most faithful to the truth.

In his book about the siege of Leningrad, Harrison Salisbury tells how subordinates risked death if they dared bring Stalin unfavorable news about the war with Germany. Because of his self-imposed insulation against reality, Stalin made many strategic mistakes. It is well known that Hitler, too, chose the path of self-delusion.

Truth is costly. But self-deceit costs even more. It is a tragic mistake to demand that our heralds (newsmen or clergymen) entertain rather than inform us. Yet, there are indications that Americans are becoming weary of exposure to the turmoil of our time. As was demonstrated in Chicago, many seem to resent having it told like it is. We cannot hope to solve the complex problems of violence—in the streets or on the campus—until we first thoroughly understand them.

Some of our simplistic solutions have all the profundity of W. C. Fields' famous insomnia cure: Get plenty of sleep. We would, perhaps, like to write off much of our current disorder as nothing more than rabble-rousing by a handful of hard-core radicals. We would brand the students as communists and the black militants as criminals. That would be the easy way, for it would simultaneously spare us the agony of having to think and relieve us of responsibility.

Such self-deception in these critical days would be both silly and suicidal. Despite the excesses of some young revolutionaries, the campus set articulates some legitimate complaints against society. Despite the questionable methods of some militants, the impatience and unrest in the ghettos is not only justified but long overdue.

The issues of how men live and how they ought to

live are coming into focus. The radicals may not always have the right answers, but they are raising the right questions. Those who have fared well under the old order are upset at the challenge from those who have not. It is so much easier to denounce those outside the system than to include them. It is cheaper to curse the protestors than to correct inequities. But Christians must not succumb to either the easy or the cheap way. It is not an exaggeration to say that the salvation of our society depends upon the collective response of the committed.

When so many of man's institutions seem to be crumbling under the weight of their own obsolescence and irrelevance, that fellowship we call the church is challenged to heal, to reconcile, to save men from each other and from the heat of their own selfish desires.

Donald Brewer is one of the coolest cats around. Not every minister would consider such a description complimentary—but it fits Brewer, pastor of a church in Girard, Pennsylvania.[8]

Brewer is a magician, a clown. He can balance swords, poles, and a unicycle on his chin. His wife has four poodles and a dog act. Sometimes she flies merrily on the trapeze.

Donald Brewer has been a circus buff for a long time, longer than he's been a clergyman. Now he's found a way to combine his love of the circus and his love for people into a unique and meaningful ministry. Last year, during their summer vacation, Brewer, his wife, Melody, and their two young daughters, traveled with a circus through central Pennsylvania. They performed twice a day, six days a week, without pay.

There was plenty of compensation, though. Brewer left the big top, knowing he had brought meaning and concern to many lives where there had been little of either. He tried to help in all kinds of ways. When he wasn't acting as sideshow manager, announcer, or doing his balancing act, Brewer was making himself available for counseling, or just listening. He never held services. It was not the church but Christ he brought to the circus. Brewer let the circus folks know he cared about them and about their problems. He didn't try to *sell* God, but he readily answered their questions about God.

"Circus folks long have thought that the church looks down on them, and that's wrong," Brewer says. "I'm just filling the gap the church left unfilled for a long, long time."

Stories like this are exciting; for they tell how the ministry of Christ is moving today out of the cathedral and into the cacophony of life. Out of the sanctuary and into the shopping center. Out of the church house and into the coffee house. Out of the pulpit and into sick society with its desperate need of Jesus' message and his compassion.

There is no denying that religion appears dull and drab to some people. That's not God's fault. It's ours. The life that practices the principles of Jesus and really mirrors his concern will be a dynamic, exuberant, creative, and purposeful testimony to life at its inspired best.

One of the biggest tasks facing this generation is the task of reconciling opposing views and estranged people. It is perhaps the most difficult task of discipleship. We are challenged to place ourselves in the middle of conflict and strife.

Jesus said, "Blessed are the peacemakers." He meant, good for those who get involved in the fight in order to bring about peace. One man was asked where he would look for Jesus if He were to appear in the flesh today. His answer was, "On the wall between East and West Berlin."

We, as individuals, may not reconcile the differences between Washington and Moscow, but we may be able to resolve the dispute between two of our friends. We, personally, may not end hostilities between Israel and her Arab neighbors, but we may be able to strengthen the peace and harmony of our own neighborhood—or our own social group. You and I may feel powerless to settle that tragic war between Nigeria and Biafra, but we may build bridges of understanding between ourselves and our children.

Even such distant disputes as Arab-Israeli and Nigeria-Biafra conflicts may, ultimately, be influenced by our individual concern if we channel that concern toward those who make the policies for our own country. No one can believe that the individual voices of dissent raised by Americans against the Vietnam war have had no effect on Washington.

Christians are called to be agents of reconciliation. That means exposure to misunderstanding and hate, so that understanding and love might be brought into such situations. Christians are people who won't be looking around for the door when the kitchen gets hot. They'll simply loosen their collars. And roll up their sleeves. And go to work.

Chapter 6

Tuned In—Or Turned Off

The hippies are right about one thing: Most people do go through life—turned off. Most never see all that's there. Nor are they able to relate accurately what they do see.

If you doubt this, just try asking five different people to describe a single event which all of them witnessed. Any lawyer will tell you how facts, like beauty, tend to be in the eyes of the beholder.

Most people live in a shadow-world: obscured by their prejudices, clouded by ambiguous thought patterns, and dimmed by the impreciseness of their communications.

I think the hippies are wrong in suggesting that marijuana or LSD is the road to reality. Any rending of the veil accomplished by narcotics is both illusionary and temporary.

But there is an acute need in our society for awareness—for knowing and being known. Do we understand what others are trying to tell us? Not only with words, but in subtler ways? Are we able to get our ideas across to others, accurately? meaningfully?

It is a big challenge to communicate in a world filled with so much noise and so little understanding. A world where everybody seems to be talking and nobody seems to be listening. A world that is largely—turned off.

Let's look at the generation gap. Isn't it a breakdown in dialogue as well as a debate over direction? There are, of course, real and significant differences between parents and children. But the gap is magnified when semantical differences are added to those of substance. In other words, the breach could be narrowed simply by building better bridges of communication.

To cite a personal example: My parents and I understand each other fairly well. We don't always agree, but we do discuss our opinions. There is healthy give and take. Sometimes my ideas are altered. Sometimes I believe mother and dad change some of theirs. The point is that we maintain a wholesome respect for each other by keeping the communication lines open.

In contrast, many of my contemporaries tell me they find it impossible to discuss serious matters with their parents. One word leads to another, the next word leads to an argument, and none of the words leads to any understanding. Since the difference in age between them and their parents is similar to that between me and my parents, it is obvious that the term *generation gap* doesn't tell the whole story.

To carry the illustration further, I know people my own age with whom it is virtually impossible for me to communicate. Here is no generation gap—but a communications chasm.

Communications is much more than simply an exchange of words. After all, as a college professor once told his class, words are simply little buckets that carry thoughts. Unfortunately, the way we mishandle them, they sometimes arrive at their destination empty.

A certain congregation was about to vote on a motion to buy new chandeliers for the sanctuary. One elderly man rose from his pew at the back of the church and declared, "Folks, I'm agin' buyin' them chandeliers. In the first place, I can't spell 'em. In the second place, I don't like 'em. And besides that, what this here church needs is some new lights." Could it be the younger generation and the older generation are sometimes saying the same thing without realizing it?

Dr. Michael Novak claims the students he meets—especially the brighter ones—are quite receptive to the idea of a reality higher than the physical world perceived by the senses.[1] That might come as quite a shock to an older generation that's come to think of its offspring as apathetic if not outright hostile toward God. And that's precisely the rub.

Dr. Novak says these kids are "turned off" by the *word*, God. He says that word's been ruined for many of them by the way politicians have used it, and the way some churchmen have used it.

"It's like the word *love*," he says. "You have to go around by indirection when you're talking about God."

Novak says when he talks about meditation, or contemplation, his classes come alive. Students hang on every word. They seem to know exactly what he's talking about.

For one thing, Novak senses that college students have become disenchanted with science as a solution to the world's ills. Increasingly they seem to be concerned with spiritual values.

Novak believes the campus set recognizes its need for some kind of faith—that is, a system of belief that's not susceptible to proof. Without that, they seem to know life will have little or no meaning.

Religious labels don't interest them much. "They feel it is more important to do the thing than to say what you are doing," he says.

A somewhat inebriated man reportedly was wandering down State Street in Chicago when he asked a passerby, "Mishter, where am I?" The passerby said, "You're at the corner of State and Madison," to which the drunk replied, "Never mind the details, buddy. What city?"

Young people today are asking the big questions. They aren't asking whether the United Methodists are right, whether the Catholics are right, whether the Church of God is right. They're asking the "gut" questions. Is there a God? Is he knowable? Does it make any difference? Does life have meaning? Purpose? Does man have a future?

The message that communicates with these kids will be a message that socks at the main issues instead of finger-walking around the details.

It is self-defeating to answer questions people aren't asking. One evening a magazine salesman knocked on our door. He was a young man, apparently fresh out of magazine-selling school, if there is such a place. Anyway, he had his magazines fanned out, and his spiel down pat. Glancing over the publications while he was going through an obviously memorized speech, I decided there were two I'd like to buy. I tried to tell him so but he didn't stop talking long enough to listen. It was almost as though he'd been programmed to run through that monotonous sales pitch, and so he proceeded to talk himself right out of a sale. By the time he'd fnished describing all the magazines I was not going to buy, I was out of the mood to buy any.

Has the church been guilty of this? Have we insisted on running through creeds and dogmas like preprogrammed evangelists, determined to make every last word and punctuation heard whether there was a market for it or not? And in the process, have we managed to oversell some potential customers right out of the kingdom of God?

Communication is a lot more than talking. It's listening. We Christians had better open our ears as well as our mouths. What is modern man trying to tell us?

One thing people have been trying to tell us for a long time is that not all truth is valuable. A simple for-

tians could take some pointers from his sermons. He always spoke in direct, simple sentences. Parables. Stories. Contemporary and colloquial speech. These were his tools. And Jesus was the most effective communicator the world has ever known.

Of course his words sound strangely old-fashioned and even vague if we've seen them only in the King James Version. But they were very hip when he spoke them. And the people he talked to knew exactly what he was talking about. He didn't try to bowl them over or push them under with a lot of technical jargon he'd dug up from ancient scrolls. Jesus told it like it was. And he told it so that his audience got the message. Read the new and perhaps most contemporary version of the New Testament, *Good News for Modern Man.* That book is experiencing a sales bonanza in New York City and all over the country, because it puts old thoughts into new buckets (words) and they come through loud and clear.

Or, read J. B. Phillips' paraphrase of Paul's letters, and of the gospels. We have a motto at ABC news—and it's a good one. The motto is "Write like people talk." Well, that's how J. B. Phillips has rewritten the words of Paul, and of Jesus. The way people today talk. How refreshing to see the gospel come alive, to see it take on new relevance as it sheds archaic language that so often stands as a barrier between man and an understanding of God.

Since *Good News for Modern Man* appeared nearly three years ago, it has become the best-selling book in the history of the world. Sales at last count were more than 16 million copies and climbing.

In our attempts to converse with those outside the Christian fellowship, must we cling fanatically to such words as "salvation" and "redemption" in trying to describe the gift Jesus brought to men? He used a much simpler word. Life. Aren't there more meaningful ways of communicating this fantastic thought than through words which, by and large, have lost their meaning in our world?

Strange how the very people most apt to denounce false idols will make idols of certain words. There's nothing sacred about a word.

I learned from my aunt, Vera Martin, a missionary to Kenya, that some words which are perfectly respectable in the United States are used as profanity in Africa. You see, no *word* is good or bad, holy or profane. It's the thought the word carries. If we could stop worshiping at the altar of language, perhaps we could recapture the vitality and the crispness of the gospel, through a whole new set of expressions. As a professional communicator, I believe it's worth a try.

Am I exaggerating the problem? Then think about this: A short time ago, for one of my news reports, I interviewed one of the wealthiest men in America. I asked this multimillionaire if he believed in immortality. He said he wasn't sure what that meant. I then asked him if he believed in a life after death. He said, "Yes, I certainly do."

I couldn't care less whether that man calls it immortality or life after death. I am quite concerned about my ability to communicate with him, or anyone else, on the subject.

Then there's this business of prayer. What is prayer, anyway? We say it's talking with God, but we don't always pray like it is. Remember that Jesus condemned the kind of ostentatious prose practiced by the Pharisee. He praised the short and simple prayer of the publican. It didn't have all the thees and thous, but it had a lot of sincerity. The Pharisee seemed to be showing off and putting his piety on display. The publican had some guilt he needed to get off his chest. One was oratory—the other was prayer.

Instead of so much phony talk about invoking, and beseeching, and imploring, and supplicating, why can't we just tell God, "Look, Lord, we've got some pretty big problems around here and we've got to have help. Show us the way; we can't make it alone."

I suppose there are times when our prayers are necessarily said more for the effect they'll have on the listener than on God.

I was covering a campaign speech by Vice-President Hubert Humphrey during his 1968 bid for the presidency. It was a street rally in midtown New York. Usually New York's policemen have treated reporters exceptionally well, and I was a bit surprised and finally miffed when a couple of burly bluecoats began shoving me back toward the barricades and away from where the Vice-President was speaking.

I had been describing the rally into my tape recorder, and as the shoving increased, I began describing the "police brutality" and even reading off one policeman's badge number into my microphone. I knew that part of the tape would never be used on the air. In fact, I had no intention of even submitting it to our editor. My description was strictly for the benefit of the men around me—namely, the policeman. It worked. The shoving stopped. We continued covering the rally, close-up.

I suppose when we're opening a legislative session, or a race track, or inaugurating a President, the prayer is presumed to be primarily for the ears of the audience. But I'm talking more about private prayer. The kind that communicates between an individual and God. The kind that demands we listen as well as speak.

What it all adds up to is this: The day of the conditioned response for the church is over. We must not be like Allen Selverston's dog, Thor.[2] Thor was a German

Shepherd who'd been trained always to come immediately when Allen called. One day, while Allen was visiting Stanford University, Thor managed to get onto the tile roof of a four-story biology lab. As Allen left the building, he spotted Thor on the roof and automatically whistled. Thor responded immediately—and leaped four floors to his death.

The church must stop responding with a pat answer every time someone whistles a question our way. We've got to stop, look, and think before we leap. People today, especially young people, expect—even demand—reasoned responses from the church.

Sermons must be more than entertainment. William Davis, editor of *Punch,* says, "The kind of humor I like is the thing which makes me laugh for five seconds and think for ten minutes."

Are we making people think as well as smile? Are we forcing them to reevaluate, to analyze, to come to terms with their own concepts and ideas about God, and life, and others?

We may never be perfect communicators. Dwight L. Moody, the famous evangelist, was approached by an English teacher who claimed she'd counted seven grammatical errors in his sermon. "Don't you think that's a lot?" she asked.

"Yes," Moody replied. "Probably I made even more than that. But," he continued, "I make my mistakes in the service of Jesus Christ. How are you making yours?"

No matter how well we communicate, some won't listen. The International Flat Earth Society still insists the world is flat, despite all those pictures our Apollo astronauts have taken of it. Sam Shenton, head of the society, admits he's lost a lot of members as a result of those pictures, but says he's not convinced.

So I suppose, as Jesus himself said, even if someone

were to come back from the dead there are those who would not believe. Still, we must try. We must be certain their unbelief is not the result of our bungling. If some do not believe, let it be in spite of clear communication, not because of bad communication.

Chapter 7

Freedom Now

Looking up at my library shelves I see a book entitled *Freedom and Responsibility in Broadcasting*. Nearby is another book called *A Free and Responsible Press*.

It is no accident that the words freedom and responsibility often appear together. It is proper to pair them, for responsibility is the price of freedom. This is true whether we consider freedom in the theological or in the political sense. It is true whether we view freedom in the personal or in the social context.

To be free is to be responsible. To be irresponsible is to forfeit freedom. True freedom does not bring exemption from reasoned, disciplined conduct. It is not license for special privilege. Freedom does not mean destruction of or disregard for the rules.

Freedom is, in a real sense, doing what we want to do. It is being what we want to be. But no one can do nor be all that he wants without practicing the disciplines of freedom.

Few subjects are more timely today, for people everywhere demand freedom and they demand freedom Now. It is a legitimate demand because man was made to be free. The urgency and universality of the demand are both understandable, for the spirit of man needs freedom as the lungs of man need air.

To understand the depth of man's need for freedom is to understand why men have spent their lives and given their lives in its pursuit. Far better minds than mine have devoted years and volumes to the task of defining freedom and explaining it. I do not presume in these brief pages to offer a comprehensive or authoritative study on freedom.

Rather, I want to share some personal thoughts and observations about this very big and very important word. Freedom, like love, is a word badly tarnished by misuse and badly distorted by misunderstanding. Still, the concept it represents is too vital to ignore. Freedom should be one of the first words in the Christian vocabulary.

It is good to declare freedom, to proclaim it, to demand it. But life's most meaningful qualities cannot be obtained simply by verbalizing them. Freedom, like love, is not purchased by statement alone. To paraphrase an old spiritual, "Everybody talkin' 'bout freedom ain't goin' there."

Fundamental to an understanding of freedom is recognition that it is a process. Freedom may be modified by words such as *more* and *less*. Freedom is not an absolute condition. Like love it is contextual and, like love, refers as much to relationship as to an entity.

Life imposes upon all men certain limitations which preclude absolute and total freedom. Some societies are more free than others. Some individuals are more free than others. All individuals experience more or less freedom during the course of their lives as both their capacities and circumstances change.

To demand or expect complete and ultimate freedom in this life is to invite disillusionment. Neither individuals nor nations can be unconditionally free. Individuals and nations can be continually enlarging and extending freedom.

Just as the intellectual potential of the human mind is incalculable, so the human spirit's capacity for freedom is immeasurable. It is this limitless nature of freedom which challenges man constantly to refine it.

When I was first married, my mother-in-law told me how love between husband and wife can grow with the passing years. As a newlywed, I could not comprehend ever loving my wife more than at that moment. Now, fifteen years later, I am beginning to understand. Our love has indeed deepened and strengthened. With the birth of our son, in 1965, came even greater insights into the mysterious infinity of love. Who can fully fathom love's growth potential?

So it is with freedom. The more we practice it the more we understand it. The more it increases the more we recognize its limitlessness.

Anyone who boasts of absolute freedom is at best intellectually confused, at worst morally arrogant. As a newsman I hope I am more free today than I was a year ago; more free of prejudice, of incompetence, of fear and timidity. I believe I am experiencing progressively greater freedom to be a good reporter. I do not now nor do I ever expect to claim absolute freedom as a journalist, for I will always be constrained both by external pressures and internal inabilities. I can constantly cultivate and accelerate the freedom process.

As a Christian I hope I am more free today than I was a year ago; more free of self-centeredness, of hatred, of apathy, and insensitivity. I believe I am finding greater freedom to be a whole person. I do not now nor do I expect—in this life—to be an absolutely free being, for my moral capacities are limited and my motives are not always pure. I can move steadily along the path of renewal and reform toward that final freedom which every Christian believes will be ultimately his. For, as the late Roy Burkhart put it, the ultimate freedom is the freedom from death.

If freedom is a process and not a *fait accompli,* it is also a means and not an end. Freedom poses the question "For what?" Freedom is active, not passive. Freedom invites—even demands—a response. Freedom to destroy? Freedom to build! Freedom to steal? Freedom to share! Freedom to cheat? Freedom to love! Freedom to create problems? Freedom to solve them! You see, freedom *from* should always be thought of in terms of freedom *for.*

The Random House Dictionary of the English Language gives seventeen definitions for freedom. Two of them, it seems to me, are sufficient to describe freedom's essence:

First, "exemption from external control [or] interference. . . ."

Second, "power of determining one's . . . own action. . . ."

These two definitions summarize freedom as it relates to modern man. The first defines freedom in the social setting. The second defines freedom as it pertains to the individual. Man's struggle for freedom is a dual quest: he seeks freedom from others and freedom from self.

Our experiences confirm the value of both freedoms. Daily we confront both other-imposed and self-imposed obstacles to expression and accomplishment. Daily we find our progress and development inhibited both by society's shackles and those which bind our own souls.

Christianity recognizes and addresses itself to both brands of bondage. It is the Christian's contention that individuals and society should progress, simultaneously and interdependently, toward freedom. It is a cyclical process; that is, as I find greater personal freedom, I help make society more free. Conversely, as society evolves toward greater liberty, my prospects for individual freedom are enhanced.

The Christian, therefore, wages a relentless struggle against those characteristics of his personality and ego which would enslave him as well as against the unjust requirements of society. Freedom, as Jesus taught it, means freedom from self and freedom from others. To put it into biblical terms, it is freedom from sin and freedom from slavery.

This does not, however, imply freedom from responsibility. Freedom comes from cooperation with the laws of life. It is not the product of opposition to them. If we were to devise an equation for stating freedom in mathematical terms, it probably would be: Knowledge plus dicipline equals freedom. Such a formula is simple to illustrate.

Since the dawn of time man has longed to fly—to break the bonds of gravity and sail the winds like a bird. I know that restless urge. I became interested in airplanes when I was fourteen and earned my pilot's license when I was nineteen. I know the exhilaration that comes from watching the earth recede beneath the wings of a small plane, the thrill of controlling one's course in three dimensions, the beauty of familiar things shrinking below the horizon until they merge into grand patterns and forms. I love the freedom of flying.

Of course that fascinating feeling of having conquered gravity is illusionary. Gravity is never conquered. Airplanes fly because they are built and operated according to nature's laws, not in violation of them. Airplanes stay in the air because the science of aerodynamics is understood, not because it is ignored.

The history of man's attempts to fly is a history written in blood and punctuated by tragic failure. For every pioneer aviator who added a success to that history, a score of others lost fortunes and some their lives writing chapter after chapter of broken dreams. The story of flight is not a story of nature overcome but of nature understood.

As a newsman, I've been covering the space program since the early days of the two-man Gemini flights. I recall the rendezvous of Gemini 6 and Gemini 7 in December 1965. Gemini 4 had attempted, the previous July, to rendezvous with its own Titan rocket booster but had failed. NASA conceded that Gemini 4 astronauts Jim McDivitt and Ed White had been unable to close in on their target because nobody at that time fully understood all of the orbital mechanics involved. Whenever the astronauts tried to accelerate toward the booster—as one would drive a car up to another traveling ahead of it—they only pushed themselves into a higher orbit. This widened the distance rather than narrowing it.

But scientists know very well that the pathway to knowledge is paved with the stumbling blocks of failure. So they analyzed, computed, rethought and refined their concepts of orbital rendezvous. Once they fully understood and observed the rules they were free to do as they pleased.

Failure to grasp this basic truth mars the freedom cry of modern man. Many youths seem especially reluctant to recognize that freedom is not free—it costs. Freedom does not come simply upon demand. Freedom for the individual or for society must be forged on the twin anvils of knowledge and dedication.

Jesus said, "You will know the truth and the truth will make you free." Men of perception and goodwill can hardly question youth's demand for freedom. But men of good sense are justified in questioning the maturity behind some calls for freedom. Sensitive adults must sympathize with the legitimate demands of students for freedom to improve society. But even the most committed adult is understandably appalled when the campus ultimatum seems aimed at destroying the very process of freedom. In an increasingly shrinking world where people must live in smothering proximity to each other, freedom from all regulation and responsibility would be the grossest perversion of true liberty.

The great violinist, Fritz Kreisler, was approached backstage by an enthusiastic fan who cried, "Oh, Mr. Kreisler, I'd give my life to play as you do."

Quietly he replied, "Madam, I did." Kreisler was free to perform masterpieces in a magnificent way but not because he declared his freedom to do so. It was because he understood that freedom to do as he pleased with a violin meant he first had to learn the rules and accept the rigorous dicipline of music.

Personal success, no less than scientific or artistic success, depends upon acceptance of this principle that truth and training are cornerstones of freedom. Freedom from self depends upon recognition of how enslaved we are. No one can become free who believes he is inherently free. Any expert on alcoholism will tell you that the first step an alcoholic must take on the road back to rehabilitation is to fully admit his problem. He must face the truth about his condition. Only as he begins to understand why he drinks can he begin to conquer the compulsion.

The power to overcome in life is derived largely from insight. The Christian, for instance, knows life has meaning. From this insight comes unusual strength for dealing with life. Just as freedom springs from truth, so power springs from freedom. The person who has been freed from feelings of futility and despair will find a reservoir of energy for facing life's toughest situations.

Wordsworth took note of this when he wrote:

Because the lovely little flower is free
Down to its root, and, in that freedom,
bold.

The person who practices freedom doesn't let life push him around. He knows defeat is temporary, despair is curable, and he recognizes that even death cannot destroy the man who lives in the dimension of eternity.

Medicine is beginning to discover what Jesus knew about the relationship between health and attitude. Doctors know that physical and mental wellbeing are intrinsically linked. I have seen people knocked flat on their backs by overpowering mental and emotional problems. And I have seen faith and confidence lift people from sickbeds and send them on their way to recovery.

I have seen faith free men from alcoholism, from compulsive gambling, from feelings of inferiority and guilt. I have seen men saved from financial failure or failure in home life because they found the Christian path to freedom. I know people who are now finding freedom from envy, from unforgiving attitudes, from hypersensitivity, from unreasonable doubts which haunt and torment and enslave.

By committing himself to a fuller understanding of himself, the Christian continually expands his area of action. He finds freedom from disorganization and wasted time. He constantly increases his prerogatives and releases his own inner storehouse of creative energy. He has learned that true freedom comes not from self-indulgence but rather from self-examination. Some have scoffed at the supposed power of positive thinking. Inevitably, the scoffers are those who have not tried it.

Nor is there any freedom with prudence and restraint. A motorist, just regaining consciousness after an accident, said to the policeman, "But I did have the right of way."

To which the officer replied. "You sure did, buddy. But he had the truck." It is commendable to insist on our rights. It is equally commendable to recognize their practical limits. As an American citizen, I am given the right of free speech. I am free to tell off my boss. But to fully exercise this privilege could impose serious restrictions on other freedoms—such as the freedom to keep my job.

If respecting the rules is a condition for an ordered life, it is no less a condition for an ordered society. But there is a significant difference between the immutable laws of nature we have just discussed and those imperfect, man-drawn regulations which we also call laws.

One cannot—and therefore should not—defy the law of gravity. One can—and therefore should—challenge that law which would punish a person because he happens to be born black or red. Or born poor.

The difference between these two laws is immediately obvious: Not only is the law of gravity beyond our capacity to change, it is also universal and, therefore, just. It applies equally to all men. The white man who jumps from an airliner at 35,000 feet altitude will be no less and no more subject to gravity's consequences than a man of any other color. Men, women, boys, girls; Negroes, Caucasians, Indians, Orientals—all are equal under the law of gravity.

As social creatures our constant aim should be to make our rules as consistent and as universal in both concept and application as the laws of nature. When any man-made law is so obviously unfair or unjust it inflicts harm—physical or mental—upon any segment of society, we should engage that law in a battle to the death.

Of course, there are those who will argue that Christians are obligated to obey all laws, including the most grievous impositions of greedy and self-centered men. This is nonsense. That civil disobedience can be a virtue is clearly shown in the Bible, from the refusal of three young Hebrews to bend before an earthly head of state, to Jesus' refusal to answer Herod's questions. The latter was a clear violation of Roman law, and Jesus had no fifth amendment to give legal sanction to his silence.

Nearly every Christian martyr from Stephen onward, could have saved his life if he had bowed submissively before the "lawful" forces of oppression. But when principle and law come into conflict, principle must take precedence. This was recognized by all the great moralists, long before the trials at Nuremburg brought the issue so startlingly into focus.

Anyone who would conclude that the way of the cross is the way of passive submission to all of man's laws should contemplate where such a conclusion leads. It would morally condemn every early Christian who met clandestinely in the catacombs. It would morally exonerate every Nazi who carried out his orders no matter how brutal or inhuman. It would censure those colonial revolutionaries who defied England to forge out a new, free society. It would excuse those who crucified Jesus under the lawful orders of the Roman regime.

To be sure, America is a nation of laws, not of men. The Christian does not quarrel with that. With all its shortcomings, the United States has produced the closest approximation yet of a truly democratic society. We are justifiably proud of the giant strides our country has taken toward liberty and justice during its brief history. This progress has been made largely because we have written progressive laws. However, to be a nation of laws, not of men, does not mean we consider laws more important than men. Not at all.

No, we must begin to see that social action is not foreign to our faith. It is basic to it. We must oppose those laws and rules which unfairly discriminate, whether *against* a minority—as in the case of black people—or *for* a minority, as in the case of oil interests with their ludicrous tax breaks.

At the ballot bax, in the legislative halls, in the courts, and if need be, on the streets, we must fight those statutes and practices which deny dignity to some or grant special privilege to others. Thanks largely to a massive and compassionate campaign in this country, waged under the banner of *freedom movement,* many of the more obviously discriminatory laws have been erased from local and state books.

But old customs crumble slowly. Old prejudices die hard. Old habits are not easy to break. It has been said that all law floats in a sea of ethics. We are responsible, then, not only to oppose bad laws, but to bring Christ's spirit into situations where good law and bad feelings collide.

The Bible teaches that Christians live beyond law. This means they are to go further than the law. Whereas the law says don't punch your neighbor in the mouth, the Christian ethic says love your neighbor. Even more, love your enemy. Whereas the law says don't run a red light, the Christian ethic says be courteous to the other driver. Be considerate. Whereas the law forces you to go that first mile in your relationships with others, the Christian ethic says go, willingly, that second mile.

This is not only basic American ideology, it is basic Christian theology. Like Joshua and his courageous-but-outnumbered band, we must march and march and march around the unjust laws and practices of our time—until the walls, all of them, come tumbling down.

Freedom is for the individual and freedom is for society. It is a quality, a state of being, a condition, and always a process. It is the right to relate to all other men on an equal basis. It is the ability to do what we please by understanding the price of that ability. Freedom is not escape from responsibility. It is the right to be responsible.

Our society offers us many opportunities for free choice. We are free to use our influence to champion any cause, or to destroy any human right. We are free to turn off things—like people, or ideas. We are free to forget, free to hurt, free to be indifferent.

We are also free to love. Free to explore life in search of excellence. We are free to master ourselves and free to commit ourselves to extending freedom to all men.

We are free to choose self-discipline, or be subject to imposed discipline. True freedom comes not to the cynics who distrust life, nor to the anarchists who demand the individual right to order the lives of other men to suit themselves. Freedom comes not to the strong-armed men who undertake to overpower life.

Freedom, like love, knows no limits. The more of it we give, the more we have.

In the warrant which Jesus took for his own ministry, he said, "He hath sent me to proclaim release to the captives . . . to set at liberty them that are bruised" (Luke 4:18, Phillips).

Jesus went about freeing men from sin, from sickness, from the bondage of futility. We should not forget his promise that we would do even greater works.

Chapter 8

Now and Forever

"Do not be afraid of men, and do not worry."
(1 Peter 3:14, TEV)

Concern for security is humanity's heritage, but modern man's concern borders on obsession. Linus has become the symbol of us all; for we all need our security blankets.

This concern for security is understandable; for modern man lives with the nightmare of instant destruction. He knows that in a moment civilization could disappear in a mushroom cloud.

Beneath this ominous danger of swift and total annihilation, man confronts other—no less fatal—realities. They range from earthquakes and floods to mass starvation and disease.

But the threat to physical life is only partly, not wholly, responsible for man's anxiety. Perhaps Walter Lippmann has correctly assessed the other aspect of the security problem for twentieth century man:

> The malady is caused, I believe, by the impact of science upon religious certainty and of technological progress upon the settled order of family, class, and community. The "virtual despair" comes from being uprooted, homeless, naked, alone and unled. It comes from being lost in a universe where the meaning of life and of the social order are no longer given from on high and transmitted from ancestors but to be invented and discovered and experimented with, each lonely individual for himself.[1]

Modern man's sense of insecurity is dual in nature. He is tormented by doubts both about the future of all mankind and about his own personal destiny. He despairs over the prospect of extinction as a race. He trembles at the certainty of his individual death.

Each anxiety amplifies the other, creating reverberations of dread and horror. These vicious vibrations are shaking modern man apart at the emotional seams. In the words of John Bright: "The angel of death has been abroad throughout the land; You may almost hear the beating of his wings."

Whether or not man can survive is not only a valid question, it is the supreme question—for unless it can be answered affirmatively, all other questions are irrelevant. Of what ultimate value is a moon landing, a cancer cure, or an end to war if *all* of man's dreams and hopes are condemned to eventual oblivion?

Jesus was very much concerned with the survivability of man. The promise of eternal life was at the heart of his gospel. He promised immortality to individuals. He promised an eternal kingdom where meaningful life could continue, collectively; for man was not meant to be alone here or in the hereafter.

Although the people of Jesus' day faced no atomic peril, they were deeply concerned with the issue of man's permanence. It was the quest for security which prompted the rich young ruler to ask Jesus, "What good thing must I do to receive eternal life?"

Centuries before Jesus' birth, the righteous sufferer, Job, articulated the question mortals have pondered in every age, "If a man die shall he live again?" To the scourges which racked Job's body and tormented his soul, contemporary man has added countless hazards. The question of human continuation is certainly no less cogent to spaceage man than it was to the ancients.

Sometimes the church is accused of ignoring present

realities in favor of future hopes. Sometimes the accusations are justified. Just as some nonbelievers seem concerned only with the here and now, some Christians seem preoccupied with the hereafter.

It seems to me whatever life is to come surely must be relevant to the life that is. Whatever future exists beyond the grave surely must be an extension of the present, not something altogether different from the life we now know—but more likely a new dimension of this existence.

Any speculation about the nature of the after-life is, of course, just that—speculation. The fact is that today is ours—tomorrow is God's. Whatever we accomplish must be done here and done now.

It is recorded that God not only made this world, he liked what he had made. He saw that it was good. He charged man with replenishing and tending it. He made man the overseer, the supervisor. Neither in the Bible, nor in logic, can a Christian find justification for ignoring earthly duties, for shrugging off the very real challenges of this very real world.

Still, there's no denying that some believers have used their religion as a shield against responsibility. Some have sought from their faith an excuse from involvement in the world's difficulties. This is not a proper Christian view, and those who would seek such escapism in their churches are living testimony to communism's most serious charge against religion: that it is an opiate, tranquilizing man against the present, harsh realities of life.

There are two ways in which the believer may seek immunity from life's obligations. One is to pretend this life does not matter, that human existence is only an ignoble burden to be borne, pursuant to the life to come. Some religions, notably Buddhism and Hinduism, do tend to discount the value of physical life. Through meditation and mysticism, they seem to aim chiefly at meticulously guiding the faithful through the maze of the present, into a higher and better order.

A second alibi for avoiding responsibility is the contention that man does not count. The believer may be tempted to accept, without modification, the message of that once popular song, "He's got the whole world in His hands"; to conclude that despite the terrible mess man has made of the world, God, of course, will come along and at the last minute straighten it all out.

From the sad shape of things, it should be evident that operationally, at least, God has put the whole world in man's hands. God has given us the options. In his book, *Sin, Sex, and Self-Control,* Dr. Norman Vincent Peale says, "Order and certainty govern nature. The moon obeys the laws of gravity. The rabbit in the road and the owl are controlled by instinct. But in the life of the human being there is nothing fully predictable, for man—man alone—can alter his environment and change his future. God has given him a will of his own and left it free."[2]

Remember that Adam and Eve, according to the biblical account, had a pretty good thing going in the Garden of Eden. But God had given them the freedom to choose. When they made the wrong choice they were required to pay a severe penalty.

The people of Noah's time brought destruction upon themselves by exercising their options—and making bad decisions. Time and time again the Israelites lost their way, spiritually and literally, because they chose unwisely.

There is little basis in the Bible or in history for supposing that whatever man does, however foolishly or selfishly he behaves, God will inevitably rush to the rescue.

We humans hold within our hands the seeds of self-destruction. If every individual has the option of suicide, then surely collective man is no less free. Nations have perished and empires have crumbled because of moral rot and spiritual decay. Destruction is one of the possibilities open to man.

In his book, *The War Business,* George Thayer notes that in the twenty-four years since 1945 there have been fifty-five wars of significant size, duration, and intensity throughout the world.

Even as I write this chapter, war rages in Vietnam, smolders in Nigeria, threatens in the Middle East, and spreads a foreboding shadow over dozens of demarcation lines from divided Berlin to the Indian-Kashmir border. World statesmen are openly fearful that one of these tension points may trigger an Armageddon.

The brilliant Russian scientist and philosopher, Andrei D. Sakharov, recognizes man's capacity for global suicide: "The division of mankind threatens it with destruction. Civilization is imperiled by: a universal thermonuclear war, catastrophic hunger for most of mankind, . . . and destruction or degeneration from the unforseeable consequences of swift changes in the conditions of life on our planet."[8]

Already the United States and the Soviet Union have stockpiled enough nuclear weapons to kill all mankind many times over. An average nuclear warhead for a modern missile could spread atomic fires over an area 150 times greater than that burned at Hiroshima. A typical warhead could totally destroy an area thirty times greater than the area laid in ruins by the Hiroshima bomb.

The power encapsulated in a single Minuteman nose cone could devastate forty square miles—literally wipe out a major city. Millions would be killed outright from the blast and fire of a single missile. Millions more would die from smoke, dust, falling debris, and radioactive fallout.

When he was secretary of defense, Robert McNamara warned: "A full-scale nuclear exchange between the United States and the Soviet Union, lasting less than one hour, would kill almost 100 million Americans—the equivalent of over 300 World War Twos. There would be little comfort in knowing that over 100 million Russians would also be killed."[4]

No committed Christian can turn away from the nuclear threat and suppose it is not his concern. No sensitive Christian can sing "This Is My Father's World" then blithely ignore the growing threat to that world posed by the arms race.

Even if man's natural bent toward war is restrained by the fear of mutual destruction, there is no denying the considerable risk of accidental holocaust.

I was a uniformed member of the Strategic Air Command in the fall of 1959 when a false warning light sent SAC bomber crews scrambling. You may recall the published accounts. It was 4:52 A.M. on November 25, that a green light went out on a panel at SAC headquarters near Omaha, Nebraska. In less than fifteen minutes, some 750 jet planes loaded with H-bombs were taxiing to runways at a hundred bases all over the world. Before the planes were airborne, SAC headquarters discovered that the light had gone out due to an overheated motor.

For more than four years, I reported on bomber and missile activities at SAC headquarters and at Vandenberg Air Force Base in California. I developed a great respect for America's failsafe procedures designed to insure against war by accident. The fact remains that no amount of precaution, no system or scheme, can take all the danger out of our world.

Yet, a general war simply is no longer an acceptable

alternative to political settlements, if indeed it ever was. In 1964, President Johnson said:

> Once—once upon a time even large-scale wars could be waged without risking the end of civilization. But what was once upon a time is no longer so, because general war is impossible. In a matter of moments you can wipe out from 50 to 100 million of our adversaries or they can, in the same amount of time, wipe out 50 or 100 million of our people, taking half of our land, half of our population in a matter of an hour. So general war is impossible, and some alternatives are essential.[5]

President Johnson was not saying that war could not happen. He was saying that war is impossible in the sense that it is no longer a method which rational men can choose.

General Thomas S. Power, my former commander, declared: "In a nuclear war there can be no winners, only losers to varying degrees."

We cannot afford to underestimate the current threat of thermonuclear conflict. China's nuclear knowhow is increasing, as is her capacity for building bombs and delivery systems. France seems determined to emerge as a credible member of the nuclear club. Despite a treaty which bans the spread of nuclar weapons, such weapons are becoming increasingly cheap—and available. They are growing in destructive power. And there is no defense against a massive rocket attack. Whatever motives of politics or diplomacy are behind the drive to construct an antiballistic missile system, the fact is, no useful system now exists nor is it likely an efficient ABM system can be devised in the foreseeable future. As a newsman with close connections inside the military establishment and the aerospace industry, I am personally convinced that the ABM is—at this stage—an unworkable concept.

Enough said about the nuclear threat. Modern man faces so many others.

Take CBW for instance—Chemical, Biological Warfare. This expensive and controversial effort has been conducted in such secrecy that even the President of the United States apparently doesn't know its full scope. One unofficial investigation estimates that about $2.5 billion have been invested—since 1960—in development of chemicals and germs to kill man, his animals, and his crops.

It is known that some 5,000 technicians are involved in a network of military laboratories, arsenals, and test areas across the country. They are busily researching, developing, and laying away or maintaining ready production lines for gas and germ weapons. Until recently, secrecy has severely limited congressional debate over CBW.

No one seems to know exactly how much poisonous gas and other lethal agents the U.S. has stockpiled. But it apparently runs into millions of pounds.

A long overdue review of chemical and biological experimenting was finally begun primarily because of an accident in 1968. An airplane spread out a cloud of nerve gas which missed its test zone at Dugway Proving Ground in Utah and killed thousands of sheep on a nearby ranch.

Can man survive? Only if the major world powers can find some means of living together without war. Only if the nuclear powers can find some way of permanently defusing their differences—some way of working within a cooperative framework in which problems are jointly resolved.

Ours is, indeed, one world. To deny it is as pointless as to deny that the world is round. Events in the remotest corners of the world can have a direct effect upon our lives, our safety, and our taxes. Satellites have made instant communications possible between farflung capitols of the world. Astronauts and cosmonauts can circle the earth several times in a single day. Supersonic transports soon will put New York and Tokyo within commuting distance.

Barbara Ward has written a book entitled *Spaceship Earth* in which she likens the world to a spacecraft on a journey through the cosmos. It is an accurate analogy, for we do ride together on this "fragile chunk of granite," as astronaut Frank Borman described the earth during Apollo 8's flight home from the moon. Just as no first-class passenger on an airliner can be unconcerned about a fire in the tourist section, so the privileged nations of the world cannot afford indifference to the plight of underdeveloped countries.

We must face the threat posed by hunger and overpopulation. We must pay attention to what's happening in the poorer half of our world. True, the world's food production has increased 70 percent over the past thirty years, while population has grown by only 50 percent. But the balance between population growth rate and food production rate has not been favorable in underdeveloped regions.

In India, Indonesia, numerous countries in Latin America, and in parts of Africa, the situation is worsening and appears destined to continue worsening. Many of these countries lack both the technology and the economic reserves to fully utilize their resources. Some are so backward in their culture and so void of competent leadership that, without outside help, their spiraling birthrates inevitably will produce disaster.

There are many other reasons for modern man to feel insecure. We face potential catastrophe because of the way we are changing the natural balance of our world. We poison the atmosphere and the water with chemicals. We indulge in the indiscriminate use of pesticides.

We cannot even guess at what point we will cross the line between danger and disaster. We dump radioactive wastes and detergents into rivers and streams, permit erosion of our earth by cutting down forests on mountainsides, destroy birds and other wildlife, seemingly with regard only for economical and political interests. In a real sense, man has become his own worst enemy.

For those of us living in urban areas there are added reasons for alarm. A high ranking United Nations diplomat says this about living in New York City: "There is a fear hanging all over New York over crime in the streets. I hate to mention law and order; to me it sounds racist. Yet, who is not for law and order, black or white, especially when we have to *walk* down a lonely street at two in the morning? The only one who is not for it is the criminal himself."[6]

Even our homes no longer provide sanctuary. Break-ins have become so widespread in New York that the city has launched an anticrime crusade under the tongue-in-cheek banner Support Your Local Burglar.

Nor can we feel confident about the products we buy. A confidential report, written by the Food and Drug Administration, makes chilling reading for American consumers. I saw the report's conclusions, a copy of which had been obtained by United Press International. In essence, the report claims the federal government is doing a grossly inadequate job of protecting consumers from dangerous drugs, contaminated food, and other hazardous products. It details how pesticides, flammable fabrics, electrical appliances, and other potentially hazardous products for household use cause an estimated 18,000 deaths and 20 million injuries annually.

"The past twenty-five years," it says, "have witnessed an enormous increase in the number of potentially hazardous products introduced into the average American home. The consumer literally is surrounded by an arsenal of products which can kill or maim him."[7]

Undoubtedly the availability of information such as the FDA Report is compounding modern man's sense of insecurity—for never in history have men been confronted with such a volume of facts and statistics about life's dangers.

Our communications media constantly remind us that life is a minefield, filled with a myriad of threats to health and safety. We are warned that smoking causes cancer, that obesity contributes to heart attacks and other diseases, that speed on the highway kills, that sitting too close to the color television set can subject us to harmful doses of radiation. Modern man is a jittery jumble of short-circuited nerves, tiptoeing timidly through life encumbered by an inventory of fears which range from taxes to death—from inflation to infection.

Perhaps one of my graduate school professors at Northwestern, Baskett Mosse, spoke something of a proverb when he told our journalism class: "The only security you'll ever know in this erratic news business is what you carry around in your head." I suspect the only security any person can know in this life is what he carries within himself. The psalmist sensed this truth: "Thou, Lord, only makest me dwell in safety" (Ps. 4:8).

Such assurance is still possible even in this apprehensive age. Consider the case of Ron Frederickson. Ron was only thirty years old when doctors told him his kidney condition, and the diabetes which caused it, would be fatal. A few months ago, at the age of thirty-three, Ron Frederickson lay dying in a Minneapolis hospital. By this time he was blind, his body ridden with pain. But Frederickson told his young wife, Karen, he was ready to die.

And, in an interview with a columnist for the Minneapolis Star, Frederickson said: "I tell you I'm not afraid of death. Do you know how I feel? I'm kind of excited. Some time ago I became what I think is a real Christian. I now really believe this is just a beginning."

Of course the skeptic is quick to regard such optimism as a false sense of security, evolved from fear. The skeptic is quick to see in such deathbed confidence only the fantasizing of a desperate man. He considers it a thought born of a wish rather than of reason.

It is true that one cannot achieve such confidence strictly by reasoning. On the other hand, such tranquility does not come simply by wishing for it. The *philosophy* of Christianity does have an appeal to man's intellect—for reason does acknowledge that love is better than hate, that hope is better than despair, that life is better than death. Christianity also has an emotional appeal, for man does wish to survive.

But neither reasoning nor wishing can produce the certainty which enables some to walk calmly—almost easily—through the valley of death. Such certainty is born of faith—that uniquely human quality which does not defy facts but which is more than facts. For faith recognizes that reality is bigger than man's grandest abilities to perceive it. Faith is facts plus intuition, insight, inspiration, and emotion. It is the ability to believe more than can be proven.

To be a believer is to be a spiritual Columbus. It is to declare confidence that the world is round when all the hard-nosed realists can clearly see that the world is flat. Belief is the ability to see beyond the known world to the world which can be known.

A valid faith must be built upon a solid foundation of logic. But intellect is only the starting point for faith. When America's space planners decided a decade ago to put men on the moon, they were branded dreamers by many. To be sure, they were. But their dreams were extensions of reason, not opponents of reason. Their belief that astronauts could be walking on the moon before 1970 was unprovable. Some of the skills and materials needed for such a venture had yet to be developed. Nonetheless, their confidence did not defy what was known, it simply went beyond what was known.

So it is with the Christian's faith. No one can prove that the life of the individual continues beyond the grave. But is it less logical to presume man can live again than to acknowledge that he lived in the first place? Life itself is an unfathomable miracle. Even if science is successful in creating a form of test-tube life —and I do not doubt this will happen—it will in no way diminish the mystery of life. It will simply mean that man has unlocked one more secret of *how* life functions. He will have added not a particle to his understanding of *why*.

As surely as NASA's faith in moon flight was justified, I believe Ron Frederickson's faith in the continuation of life will prove well-founded. I readily concede the difficulty modern man encounters as he attempts to deal with the issue of faith. We seem to be passing through a phase where many would limit reality to those expressions of it perceivable through the five senses. In accepting as real that which we touch, taste, smell, hear, and see, must we deny the existence of those realities which may be beyond such perception?

Were X rays unreal—nonexistent—before man devised the means to discover them? Were distant stars, only recently detected on radio telescopes, not real until man knew they were there? By now, atheism should be totally unacceptable to a scientific age accustomed to seeing yesterday's heresies become today's dogmas.

The Christian does not wait for all the laboratory reports to be in before declaring his faith. Like Thomas Jefferson, we hold some truths to be self-evident. The

Christian agrees with Louis Pasteur, who said of his theories: "If someone tells me that in making these conclusions I have gone beyond the facts, I reply: 'It is true that I have freely put myself among ideas which cannot always be rigorously proved. That is my way of looking at things.'"

Faith is the Christian way of looking at things. It is not in conflict with the way science looks at things. Albert McCombs writes:

> Science brings about an insight into the majesty and omnipotence of the Supreme Being which grows stronger with each new discovery. Science replaces the paganistic superstitions, which often creep into our religious beliefs, with sound facts which can be supported by demonstrable evidence. Just as the discoveries of science have altered the practice of medicine from the days of blood letting and incense burning to our modern techniques of diagnosis and treatment, some of our ancient concepts of God's relationship to man have been altered by scientific discoveries.[8]

Serenity in the face of death—this is the ultimate security. It is available to all men but misunderstood by so many. It is what Jesus had in mind when he told his followers: "Peace I leave with you; my own peace I give you. I do not give it to you as the world does. Do not be worried and upset; do not be afraid" (John 14:27).

Man, indeed, has a need to survive. The search for the fountain of youth has not ended. At least a dozen dead persons right now repose in refrigerated coffins around the United States, put there in the hope that one day they can be brought back to life. In life they were members of the cryonics cult, a group which believes that within twenty-five years, freezing of the dead will liberate man from the inevitability of death.

Cryonics comes from the Greek word *kryos* (ice cold), the low temperature science of *cryogenics* (familiar to space buffs), and *cryobiology,* the study of the effects of temperature on living material. The idea is to freeze the body—sort of place it in a state of suspended animation—until some future time when science will have learned how to cure the disease that killed it and then reanimate it.

Whatever hope cryonics holds for extending human life beyond the normal range of years, it is not the final answer to the supreme question. There is a Christian answer—one which forges a divine assurance between the concerns of now and the covenant of the future. It is not obsession with preserving the human body, but confidence in the survivability of the human spirit. It finally comes to a man not through debate and speculation, but through commitment. That is how the late Dag Hammarskjold found the answer: "at some moment I did answer *Yes* to Someone—or Something—and from that hour I was certain that existence is meaningful and that, therefore, my life, in self-surrender, had a goal."[9]

As a world statesman—as secretary general of the United Nations—Hammarskjold played out a meaningful role on this earthly stage against a backdrop of eternal verities. Hammarskjold's confidence in ultimate meaning did not lessen his consecration to immediate concerns. Rather, such confidence gave meaning to the present.

Paul Tillich saw clearly this relationship between ultimate security and the uncertainty of the moment: "Providence means that there is a creative and saving possibility implied in every situation, which cannot be destroyed by any event. Providence means that the daemonic and destructive forces within ourselves and our world can never have an unbreakable grasp upon us, and that the bond which connects us with the fulfilling love can never be disrupted."[10]

Christians must not make their faith in the future an occasion for uninvolvement with the present. This world is real. This life has value. We can effect changes in the course of history by first being changed, then committing ourselves to solving the profusion of problems which threaten not only the quality of human life, but life itself.

Any action we take to reduce tensions is a sacrament. Any word we speak to dilute the climate of violence is a prayer. Any move we make to minimize man's differences is a fulfillment of our sacred trust. And any failure to heal those divisions which menace mankind is nothing short of criminal negligence.

It is imperative that young people with heads full of idealism and hearts full of commitment dedicate their lives to serving society; as legislators, as journalists, as members of state and defense departments, as teachers, doctors, lawyers, ambassadors. Science and industry provide unprecedented challenges to those who would forge a new and better world. The theater and the arts today often seem bankrupt of faith, and incapable of inspiring hope and confidence. How critical is the need for Christian writers, producers, and actors. The arts are not to be condemned for telling it like it is. But is there no room for creative expressions of how it ought to be? Is there no place on the stage and on the screen for courage and assurance?

Our world needs young people who will demand a rearranging of priorities. America needs to be goaded and prodded into making the kinds of investments in backward countries which may curtail America's own economic growth rate. Such sacrificial giving is justified for it is required to preserve mankind and to prevent the destruction of civilization itself.

Do not think such idealism is dead. Besides the millions of altruistic youths who openly admit their concern, I believe there are today millions of well-motivated adults; people who mask their concern, for fear of seeming unsophisticated.

Getting to know people is a good way of getting to know how many good people there are in the world. New York City supposedly is peopled by unconcerned, uninvolved, self-seeking and self-centered egoists whose dominant religion is power and whose supreme diety is wealth. Would it surprise you to learn that some of the most committed, concerned, and involved people I know are New Yorkers?

The news business is supposed to be a haven for cynics, a citadel for hard-nosed critics whose tools are sarcasm and whose pens and typewriters drip with pessimism. Would you be shocked to learn that some of the most idealistic and compassionately human people I know are newsmen?

Many of these concerned and idealistic individuals do not profess the Christian faith, though they may share the Christian point of view.

I remember, as I observe their sincere regard for others, how it was with Jesus' first followers. He was a man for others and he called his companions into a coalition of the committed.

His test of discipleship was not an intellectual examination. No true or false quiz. Not all of his followers thought alike or believed alike.

They were bound not by dogma but by their shared and selfless concern. There was diversity in their opinions, but unity in their objectives and purposes. Together this tiny band of dreamers plunged into the heat of life in a determined effort to turn the world right side up.

The job is far from finished. Leslie Weatherhead has

stated it well: "I believe that I am in the hands of a loving, wise, finally undefeatable Power whom I can call Father, and that, like every other human being, I am dear to him and cannot fall out of his hands. God is only at the beginning of his work with this planet."[11]

I share this unwillingness to give up on God's world. I do not expect God to perform man's work. I do, however, see meaning in that work because of God. There is within me a stubborn, Christian optimism which insists the best is yet to come.

Notes

Preface

1. Ernest Harrison in the foreword to Pierre Berton's *The Comfortable Pew* (Philadelphia: J. B. Lippincott, 1965), p. 26.
2. Dag Hammarskjold, *Markings* (New York: Alfred A. Knopf, 1964), p. xxi.

Chapter 1

1. Associated Press dispatch.
2. Jean-Paul Sartre, *Existentialism and Human Emotions* (New York: The Wisdom Library, 1957), p. 90.
3. Martin Luther King, Jr., *I Have a Dream* (New York: Grosset & Dunlap, 1968), p. 34.
4. Quoted by Leslie Weatherhead in *The Christian Agnostic* (Nashville: Abingdon Press, 1965), p. 144.
5. From *Good News for Modern Man*, a new translation of the New Testament in Today's English Version. Copyright American Bible Society, 1966.
6. Kahlil Gibran, *The Prophet* (New York: Alfred A. Knopf, 1966), p. 78.
7. Thomas Howard, *Christ The Tiger* (New York: J. B. Lippincott, 1967), p. 154.

Chapter 2

1. From a report presented to the World Council of Churches meeting in London, England.
2. Ernest T. Campbell in *Presbyterian Life* (Philadelphia: The Westminster Press, January 15, 1969), p. 11.
3. *Ibid.*
4. United Press International dispatch.

Chapter 3

1. "Religion in American Life" feature by UPI, May 15, 1969.
2. From a speech by U Thant reported by *The New York Times.*
3. From a speech before the World Health Organization, London, January 2, 1969.
4. From an article on "Takers" in *The Reader's Digest,* July 1969.

5. AP dispatch.
6. From *The New York Times,* August 12, 1968.
7. AP dispatch, April 4, 1969.
8. UPI dispatch.

Chapter 4

1. From a speech by Steve Bell.
2. AP dispatch, June 4, 1969.
3. UPI dispatch, December 25, 1968.
4. AP dispatch, May 6, 1969.
5. The Reverend James Ault in *The Bergen Record,* Bergen County, New Jersey, July 20, 1968.
6. From the Introduction in Carl F. Burke's *God Is for Real, Man* (New York: Association Press, 1966).

Chapter 5

1. "Religion in American Life" feature by UPI, June 20, 1969
2. Russell Baker in *The New York Times,* May 15, 1969.
3. AP dispatch, May 2, 1969.

Chapter 6

1. From *The Center Magazine* (Santa Barbara: Center for the Study of Democratic Institutions, August 1969).
2. AP dispatch.

Chapter 7

1. Roger Shinn, *Tangled World* (New York: Charles Scribner's Sons, 1965), p. 89.
2. Ernest T. Campbell in *Presbyterian Life,* January 15, 1969, p. 38.

Chapter 8

1. Walter Lippman in *The New York Herald Tribune,* August 4, 1964.
2. Norman Vincent Peale, *Sin, Sex and Self-Control* (New York: Doubleday & Co., 1965).
3. Andrei D. Sakharov, *Progress, Co-Existence & Intellectual Freedom* (New York: W. W. Norton & Co., 1968), p. 27.
4. From *The New York Times,* August 14, 1964.
5. From *The New York Times,* March 25, 1964.
6. From a personal interview by the author.
7. From a confidential, undated UPI report.
8. Albert McCombs, *The Evidence of God in an Expanding Universe* (New York: G. P. Putnam's Sons, 1958), p. 165.
9. Dag Hammarskjold, *Markings,* p. xii.
10. Paul Tillich, *The Shaking of the Foundations* (New York: Charles Scribner's Sons, 1940), pp. 106-107.
11. Leslie Weatherhead, *The Christian Agnostic,* p. 214.